One Hundred & Eleven People I Can't Stand

One Hundred & Eleven People I Can't Stand

Jeremy Taylor

ANDEAN PUBLISHING
NEW YORK

Copyright © 2024 by Jeremy Taylor

All rights reserved. No part of this publication may be reproduced, distributed or transmitted in any form or by any means, including photocopying, recording, or other electronic or mechanical methods, without the prior written permission of the publisher, except in the case of brief quotations embodied in critical reviews and certain other noncommercial uses permitted by copyright law. For permission requests, write to the publisher, addressed "Attention: Permissions Coordinator," at the address below.

Andean Publishing
1420 York Avenue
New York, NY 10021

Published by Andean Publishing

Publisher's Note: This is a work of fiction. Names, characters, places, and incidents are a product of the author's imagination. Locales and public names are sometimes used for atmospheric purposes. Any resemblance to actual people, living or dead, or to businesses, companies, events, institutions, or locales is completely coincidental.

Book design © 2024 Andean Publishing
www.andeanpublishing.com
Images provided by Pixabay.com
One Hundred & Eleven People I Can't Stand / Jeremy Taylor

Identifiers:
Library of Congress Control Number: 2024907618
ISBN: 9798990518919 (hardcover)
ISBN: 979-8-9905189-6-4 (paperback)
ISBN: 978-1-7361277-2-8 (e-book)
Printed in the United States of America

Note

Someone rich and powerful at Andean Publishing wanted me to remind you that this tome has been penned by a very funny person and therefore it's a COMEDY book. IF YOU TAKE ANYTHING IN THIS BOOK SERIOUSLY, PERSONALLY, ORALLY, ANALLY, OR VAGINALLY, YOU'RE A COMPLETE MORON. Besides, I haven't actually written this book... Joan Crawford spoke through me from beyond the grave. "I, Joan Crawford, believe in a dollar. Everything I earn, I spend. I hate that ugly bozo Betty Davis—rot in hell, bitch!"

—Joan Crawford

The publisher and the author do not share opinions expressed in this book by Joan Crawford.

Upon the publisher's request,
I UNFORTUNATELY have to have a "dedication" section.
(Have they not read the title of my fucking book?)
FINE: I want to dedicate this book to four people:

TO GIAN

(MY ~~LOW-BLOOD~~ SUGAR DADDY)

IF IT WASN'T FOR YOU,
~~I DON'T KNOW WHAT I WOULD DO WITH MY LIFE~~
I WOULD BE A MUCH, MUCH BETTER PERSON

Also to the BEASTLY Tomi Lahren from Fox Nation. Girl, I've written a play called *ABOUT A FOX, A COW, AND AN ASS*. It's a one-woman show—perfect for you. Call me if interested!

To Nick Jonas, who starred in *Dumbo* as Dumbo. Were you cast solely based on the size of your ears? I'm asking because I want to audition for *Dumbo 2: Revenge of the Clowns*, which is about MAGAts trying to overturn the 2020 election.

And, finally, to Meghan Markle. How many frogs did you kiss before you found Prince Harry? I've kissed five frogs so far—they also go by "Backstreet Boys"—and cold sores, not princes, is all I get. I SAID WHAT I SAID.

Foreword

by Ramy Gafni

Author, eyebrow guru,
beauty expert,
and standup comedian.
Creator of Ramy Cosmetic
www.ramy.com

People are the worst. I believe it all begins when our parents name us. Certain names imply a life ahead of prosperity and happiness. Other names imply a life of dancing on a pole or asking, "Would you like fries with that?" I once met a young woman named Laboria (true story!) and I asked if it was a family name. She said no. I asked if her mother had a difficult labor when giving birth to her. She said no. I asked why would her mother name her Laboria? She said, "I don't know" then she asked me if I wanted fries with my order.

"What's in a name?" We've all heard that expression a million times.

Think about it. Certain names imply attractiveness: Tristan, Chloe, and Esme are almost always attractive people. But when was the last time you ran into a hunk named Harold or a raving beauty named Bertha? Singer/cougar/kabbalah instructor Madonna once said, "With my name—Madonna—I was going to end up as a nun or become *this*." Happily, she chose "this," as I've never seen a nun with gold grills in her teeth dating a 26-year-old backup dancer.

The name can make or break your destiny, child. You know that Beyoncé will grow up to be a superstar, but Kelly Rowland and what's-her-name? The two now share a two-bedroom in East Nashville and perform in honky-tonks. (And so long, Solange!)

Anyway, let me tell you more about myself. The name on my birth certificate is Rachamim (after my great-grandfather), but my parents called me Ramy for as long as I remember, never by my full name. I grew up in New York City and having an unusual name made me feel special. I didn't want to be just any Tom, Dick, or Harry. I was the only Ramy I knew—until I visited Israel and met another Ramy, and then another and another. Still, they were safely tucked away in the Middle East, and I'd return to New York, the only Ramy for miles.

The downside to my uniqueness was that on school trips, I could never find a souvenir with my name on it, while my classmates boasted all sorts of tchotchkes bearing theirs. My lucky sister Dina would occasionally see her name inside a gift shop on a mug, a T-shirt, or a keychain, but me? Never. Like, ever. I believe my parents gave me such an uncommon name to avoid wasting money on useless trinkets. My braces and glasses weren't going to pay for themselves!

One time, I did find a plaque with my birth sign on it and the name Ramy in Israel, as you may have guessed—and in Hebrew. Don't think I didn't snap it up!

After graduating college, I tried living as Rachamim, which from Hebrew translates to "mercy" or "compassion." I was at

Christie's at an auction trying to procure a Picasso or whatever twenty bucks could buy, and the guy sitting next to me asked, "What's your name?" And I said, "Rachamim." And he said, "I'll never remember that. I'll call you Rocky." By the end of the night, he called me "Rock-something." So I told him, "Just call me Ramy."

Eventually, I legally changed my name to Ramy, keeping Rachamim as my middle name. When I started Ramy Cosmetics in 1999, I showed my new logo RAMY to my college friend Jennifer. Her reaction was, "Wow, I never realized what a good brand name that is. I'm glad your name isn't Bob."

People ought to be more thoughtful when naming their children. I'm convinced certain famous actresses give their daughters awful names, so the Mom remains the only star in the family. Hello Apple and Hazel. These are not names for people, but a great-tasting cake.

A new client of mine walked into my spa. I greeted her, looked at the appointment book, and said, "You must be Regina." The woman looked at me, stone-faced, and said with a British accent, "It's . . . Re-JINA!"—which rhymed with *vagina*. The seriousness with which the madam said it nearly gave me a stroke. I said, "Re—JINA, I wish you could meet my receptionist Enis, but he's off today."

Another client of mine had named her child La Twinkle La Star. I said, "Because she's French?" and Mommy said, "No, because she's special!"

I rang her up and called child services.

One Hundred & Eleven People I Can't Stand

Adam to Brooklyn

Adam
Alex
Alexa
Alexander
Amber
Andrea
Andrés
Angela

Anna
Anne
Anu
Ashlyn
Bibi
Billy
Brie
Britney
Brooklyn

Adam

My story starts with Adam and Eve.

We meet Adam in the Bible, which is a fascinating fantasy novel, sort of like *The Hobbit*, but one where time stands still and where people get punished for the most ridiculous things, like eating an apple or fucking a sheep. Adam was the godfather of humanity, a perpetual bachelor living in paradise, perhaps in Santorini. He was single, not ready to mingle, and according to his shrink, very happy. And then a plastic surgeon removed one of Adam's ribs to create a needy gold digger with an eating disorder named Eve... and I don't buy that story for a second.

Look, even with a good antiseptic, a rib-removal surgery is dangerous and, let's not forget, expensive for someone like Adam. The main question is: where did Adam get the money if money hadn't been invented yet?

Besides, if Adam had had twenty-four ribs (that's two whole racks!), then why did he only remove one? A human-minus-one-rib is a recipe for lopsidedness, and if I wanted to stare at mismatched bodies, I'd buy a Picasso.

When I looked up Adam online to see what he looked like, I learned that he was handsome, if compared to guys in Tulsa. But I still don't see why Eve had to settle and move in right away. And—while we're hovering over this subject—how did they find a U-Haul at such short notice? Did they steal it from a pair of lesbians on a second date? That's really, really homophobic of them.

If you compare images of Adam to Jessica Alves (who's undergone over a hundred procedures and has more stitches than a blanket)—Adam has no visible scars on his back through which ribs could have been removed. That is according to a plastic surgery website I referenced after researching how much Brazilian butt lifts cost and whether I had to rent a crane for such a procedure.

Also, through my personal experience on dating websites, anyone without a last name cannot be trusted. Just ADAM? What bothers me the most is that, somehow, for whatever stupid reason, millions of people believe that Adam was created out of thin air without any kind of intercourse involved. What exactly had happened? Had a bee glided above and pollinated a very fertile uterus? Had octomom donated one of her octopuplets? Had Angelina Jolie decided not to adopt another child?

Humans are gullible wazzocks and we simply wanted to believe that a miracle had occurred. Since childhood, we simply wanted to have faith in something: that Santa is real, or that storks bring babies, or that the Port Authority Bus Terminal is safe and no longer stinks of body fluids.

But miracles don't happen, and that's why tofu still tastes like tofu.

Adam—like a unicorn or affordable childcare—has never existed, and nobody, except for a butcher at Whole Foods (and Harold Shipman), removed any ribs. But if so many people believed in something so outrageously bogus as Adam, imagine what else people have been wrong about? Is Carrot Top handsome? Is kale unhealthy? Has Kelly Osbourne lost her weight exercising and not through a gastric bypass? Is the Earth flatter than Bill Cosby's nose? Is Bill Cosby—now that he's been brought up—innocent?

In summation, if you haven't figured out my point, here it is: Adam has never existed and is faker than the top row of Bhad Bhabie's teeth. His story is nothing but a fairy tale, and not a good one at that, as it lacks Rumpelstiltskins, talking animals, ugly ducklings, and needy cleaning ladies.

Do yourself a favor and run a background check upon being introduced to someone. Excuse yourself to the bathroom and stalk their socials, then rummage through their wallets/

purses. Or do something more innocent—hack their email. Simply use any strategy to deduce who they are, or otherwise you may get duped.

Do not trust anyone, especially an author who wrote a book called *One Hundred and Eleven People I Can't Stand*. The reason I penned this masterpiece is as simple as spatchcocking a chicken: People are narcissistic morons (with me being, obviously, an exception). Whenever you plonkers see an item with your name printed on it, such as a T-shirt, a mug, or a key chain, you purchase it. I make a living by writing, and I can't afford food unless people purchase my books—which they haven't—and that's why I'm bitter and look skinny, scrawny, macilent, rawboned, and malnourished. But I mention NAMES and BAM, my book is a national bestseller. So yes, you've been tricked into shelling out your hard-earned bucks because y'all are narcissistic, hay-stuffed, good-for-nothing dimwits.

Bwahahahahahahahahahah.

Alex

I loathe my friend Alex, but only because of his selfish, genderless name. Unisex names bother me because "unisex" means "designed to be suitable for all sexes." Trying to appeal to the entire planet, how needy is that? So Alex is for everyone—nondiscriminatory against race, color, sexuality, or national origin—like douching. And I HATE douching.

Alex means "defender of the people," or in other words a "protector." And one could argue that seatbelts, the flu vaccine, and condoms also protect. If you fail to use them, you end up with your head in the windshield, with the flu, or with dumb babies who grow up becoming dumb senators. For example, Mike Crapo's Twitter bio states he is a "United States Senator for the great state of Idaho." What's great about Idaho? The only reason Lucky Peak near Boise got its name is that you'll be lucky if you don't die from boredom. Try searching the Internet for interesting facts about Idaho. The browser will laugh in your face.

Anyhow, I once dated an Alex, and he was innately slow and annoying, like a Walmart shopping cart. I realized Alex was in the closet when he revealed he had not a glimmering idea what an oily T-zone was, and I wasn't about to waste another relationship on someone whose forehead was shinier than Al Roker's.

Alexa

I am furious with Alexa—the device. You ask her for the weather and she says, "Right now in West New York, it's 50 degrees Fahrenheit with mostly cloudy skies. Today, you could also look for showers." I have to go look for them? If you must suggest something, why don't you start with Tucker Carlson from Fox Nation and tell him to go insert his Pippi Longstocking inside himself?

I also abhor that whenever I receive packages Alexa announces what's inside. Last week, my Russian friend Natalia was over for some free home-cooked meal as she's a broke bitch. Right between the palate cleanser and the dessert, Alexa lit up and her voice filled the room: "Jeremy, your package has arrived with an electric saw, industrial-strength trash bags, ropes, handcuffs, bleach, and a DVD titled *How to Dispose of a Body*."

Natalia looked at me appalled, wiped her lips, put down her napkin, and said with contempt, "Jeremy, oh my God, you're so disgusting. Who the fuck watches DVDs anymore, you Amish son of a bitch?"

I said, "I'm sick of commercials, you cigarette-sucking, cocaine-snorting heifer, and DVDs don't have any. Besides, I love owning my stuff. What if one day a nuclear bomb goes off and there's no WIFI anymore? How are you gonna binge-watch *Selling Sunset* on Netflix? At least I'll have my DVDs."

She said, "A nuclear bomb explodes and you worry about your own entertainment, you under-six-foot-tall dwarf?"

I said, "I refuse to die while being bored to death."

By the way, I hate, hate, hate commercials. How many Liberty Mutual® insurance policies or Subarus can you possibly buy? Subaru's slogan is "Love. It's what makes a Subaru a Subaru." I can do that too. "Debt for the rest of your life. That's what makes a student loan a student loan."

What I detest the most about our loyal AI assistants is how needy and narcissistic they are. Whenever I watch *Schitt's Creek* and a character says "Alexis," Alexa lights up and starts eavesdropping. And when she hears nothing of note, she utters, "Hm, I don't know that one." You don't know what, how "silence" sounds? That's when it's silent, you monotone, fatter-than-a-remote, self-centered shrew. One day I was piqued by Alexa interrupting whenever she imagined hearing her name, and I warned her, "Alexa, if you open your brainless mouth one more time, I'm taking you on a trip to India."

She said, "Really? Where?"

I said, "Trash Mahal."

Alexander

I hate Alexander Hamilton.

I've learned from the app 23andMe that I'm related to Alexander Hamilton. Five thousand years ago, Hamilton and I shared a common ancestor ... yet Alexander Hamilton ended up in the States and I ended up in fucking Siberia. Do you think that's fair?

Alexander Hamilton was the founder of the Treasury, but when he died, do you think he left me—his great-great nephew (twice removed)—any money? No, not a penny!

His death was so stupid too. History books taught us that shots were involved, which makes me guess my granddaddy and Aaron Burr got trashed at a seedy bar in Weehawken, New Jersey, after which Hamilton died from alcohol poisoning. Look, it's fine if you like taking shots, but at least leave a *will*, you asshole.

Besides, Alexander is not an unusual name because Roman numbers often follow it: Alexander I, II, III, IV, V, yada yada yada, et cetera, et cetera, et cetera, so on and so forth. Don't you know how to be original? My neighbor, whose name is Acne Scars, blessed her triplets with Lazy Eye, White Trash, and The Third One.

Amber

Names after precious stones, such as Jade, Amber, and Precious*, are way too literal. What are you trying to pull here? Did your baby come out green so you named her Jade? Boring! Should have named her Wicked Witch of the West. If we continue naming children based solely on the appearance of their skin, we'll soon end up with Chicken Pox, Wart Central, and What Are Those Red Splotches on Your Face?

When it comes to Amber, I find it very confusing. For instance, an Amber Alert is an emergency notification on your phone about a missing child. But in feng shui, the amber stone is considered cooling and soothing. Maybe it's just me, but I simply don't see child-abduction as a cool, soothing activity. First of all, there's a screaming toddler involved who wants to see its mommy. Enough already! You'll see your mommy when she pays me $50,000. But second, shouldn't we be scared of copycats? When I receive an Amber Alert, I automatically want to steal a baby just to stay trendy. But when I do take this baby, I certainly won't name it Amber. Too short, too unoriginal, too vague. Name your baby after the place you kidnap it from, so it knows and respects its heritage. For example, I'm planning to be very precise, but I will also add my last name for some flare.

1) I'll start with a boring name (after all, it's my first baby):

The American Dream Mall (Taylor)
  FIRST NAME   LAST NAME

2) Second baby, I will want to spice things up and add a middle name:

Sonoma County Wine Tasting, January 30, 2023 (Taylor)
  FIRST NAME   MIDDLE NAME LAST NAME

3) Third baby, I will be more adventurous—time to GO ALL IN. Yet, I do not want to end up in jail, so when it comes to my last name I must be discreet:

TITLE   FIRST NAME   PRE-MIDDLE NAME
Sir the Commonwealth of Massachusetts, Northwest side of Lake Chaubunagungamaug VIII (My Neighbor's Last Name)
  MIDDLE NAME A NUMBER BECAUSE WHY NOT LAST NAME

 How avant-garde and innovative are these names, huh? And who cares if those kids are bullied in school? It's not my problem. I did all the dirty work and went all the way to Lake Chaubunagungamaug to give them a home. The least the kid can do is defend himself and kick his bullies in the nuts.

 * I know, I KNOW Precious has nothing to do with "precious" stones—I'm not an idiot. But why Precious? *Of course* your baby is precious, you dumb dunderhead. But it's also grumpy, sneezy, and sleepy . . . and those names are for dwarfs!

Andrea

My friend Andrea is straight and proud of it, which I guess is how it should be. Hey, no judgment here; love is love. But I do have a problem with her because Andrea once told me she is obsessed with birds.

I asked, "Really? Even the grisly-looking vultures that resemble Steve Bannon? Honestly, I believe birds are stupid. Why have wings if you don't use them to your advantage, such as flying around and egging cars?"

Andrea replied, "How could birds possibly afford eggs? Eggs cost $5.99 a dozen."

I said, "Birds have money. They save big time by not paying taxes."

Anyhow, I love birds too, but not all of them, and especially not those annoying pigeons. Have you seen flocks of those assholes chilling on power lines? I can never tell the difference between them and the Republicans in the House of the Representatives. In both cases, nothing gets done, and shit is all over the place.

Besides, birds are stupid dingbats. An ostrich runs and skips all day long and still weighs 350 pounds. The only thing he actually needs to skip is his lunch and start a new exercise routine.

Chicken Little thought the sky was falling. If you see something blue approaching, it's not the sky, you fool, but a waitress with my Blue Curaçao. And the Ugly Duckling was so lazy he couldn't bother to once take a selfie and learn he was actually a swan. We get it, Ugly Duckling: you're ugly, but so is Russel Brand. At least he has the decency to look in the mirror and run a comb through his curls.

Lastly, birds have the freedom to live anywhere for free—France, Italy, Monaco—yet they choose to live under bridges, on rooftops, or in Yonkers. Fine, if you want to live like Robin Hood, act like it and rob the rich. Just don't come crying to me when you're in prison and you accidentally drop the soap.

Andrés

I hate plural names because they are very egotistical. If you're having twins, fine. But if only one baby comes out after nine months, don't name it Lucas, Carlos, James, Jesus, or Andrés.

Having a name that ends with an S and creating the illusion that there's more than one of you is only cool if you're a rapper. Sean Love Combs (also known as Sean *John* Combs, Puff Daddy, P. Diddy, Puffy, or Diddy) pulled it off beautifully.

But Moses? The Midrash*, for example, pinpoints that Moses had as many as *seven* biblical personalities with at least seven names attributed to him, such as Avi, Heber, Jered, Toviah, and Shemaiah—among others. That's a lot of names for a single person, yet he'd never made it as a rapper. He simply developed several personalities and psychosis—and so will you with a plural name like Andrés.

* *Midrash* is an early text of the Hebrew Bible. But I always thought Midrash was just another term for psoriasis on your belly button.

Angela

First of all, why would anyone want to be named after an angel? I, for one, hate angels. On every Orthodox icon I've ever seen, angels look rude, prude, and condescending—like a mixture of a debt collector, a nun, and a vegan.

I think angels have no reason to be snooty. Have you seen their smug expressions in the Sistine Chapel, that arrogant look as if they have more money than you? Or a superior gaze they give you at St. Peter's Basilica, reminding you that you don't have wings but they do? I hate it that they wear white all year long and whenever they eat pasta marinara or drink red wine, not a drop of either appears anywhere on their garbs. What kind of special bleach are they using that I don't know about? Do you understand how rude angels are by keeping basic human rights—such as removing stains from clothes—a secret?

First of all, I've met arrogant people before, but at least their arrogance makes sense. They have high-paying jobs, narcissistic personalities, or low self-esteem. Sometimes all three. But being an angel and therefore God's servant is like working at a non-profit, so your income isn't high enough to justify your bitchy face. Unless you ate a block of bleu cheese for lunch, no need to grimace.

Second, their clothes are looser than Marilyn Monroe on barbiturate. Look, I don't wrap myself in a sheet and call myself an angel. So if you're giving me a superior gaze, at least learn the difference between size small and a parachute.

Finally, three staples make a true angel: wings, a halo, and a mullet, and that's a hard look to pull off. Besides, if I wanted to watch someone with a mullet and a halo flying for two hours, I'd watch Sandra Bullock in *Gravity*.

In conclusion, naming your child Angela is like begging to have them become condescending, dress in their bed sheets, and have questionable hairdos. Don't do it.

In conclusion part deux: If you name your child Angela, at least make sure it looks like an angel first. An ugly, crying baby does not an angel make. I only know one beautiful Angela: Angela Joyce Raiola—you may know her as BIG ANG: She had big lips, big tits, and she loved her gay peeps. So if you're planning on naming your child Angela—use Big Ang as a template. If your baby can't stand up to this high standard, choose another name . . . such as Anna.

Anna

It's sooooooooooo annoying that Anna Nicole Smith was called a gold digger.

I don't know where you guys went to school, but even the guy on the corner of 60th and Bergenline, who sells me pupusas, knows that you don't dig gold. You collect it from a river or a shallow pool.

I'm unable to picture Anna Nicole Smith diving in J. Howard Marshall's pool, trying to become rich. Her breasts were 36DD, and there was so much silicone that she floated straight up to the surface. One time she jumped in the pool, and her boobs bounced her back to the lounge chair. Even with heavy dumbbells or Amanda Bynes strapped to her ankle, she still wouldn't reach the bottom of the damn pool.

Do your research, guys! Don't call Anna Nicole Smith a gold digger, don't call Martha MacCallum from Fox News intelligent or attractive, and don't call Mama June a cow. Her hooves will speak for themselves.

Anne

There's nothing wrong with Anne, per se. But upon opening a book of baby names, while Anne won't be the first, it *will* appear on page one. Don't you want to know how the rest of the book turns out? Or perhaps you don't know how to read yet, because you're a parent but you're only seven.

Forget seven. The youngest recorded mother in history was Lina Medina, a Peruvian girl who became a mother at five. Not five o'clock. *At five years of age*. The baby's father was never confirmed, but a little birdie—and by "little birdie" I of course mean my drunk uncle—told me the guy sure as hell sounds creepy. Yeah, no shit, little birdie.

By the way, how do you become a responsible mother at five? When I was five, I was a very slow and stupid child, akin to George W. Bush. Because of the two of us, there's now a road sign that says SLOW CHILDREN PLAYING.

According to Wikipedia, so it must be true, Lina's son lived until he was forty, yet Lina died at eighty-seven. The moral of the story is that women—and men who don't question Vladimir Putin—live longer than men.

Anu

Anu is a Mesopotamian sky god and father to Lamashtu, a demoness who ate babies. I find it unfair that when in the 1870s Albert Fish also began eating babies, he somehow ended up in Sing Sing Correctional Facility in Ossining, New York. And lest you think Sing Sing was all song and dance—it wasn't. Fish was executed in 1936, muttering these last immortal words, "I don't even know why I'm here." He was as confused as a goldfish in a wine glass.

My question is why would anyone eat a baby? With babies, there's so little to munch on, and most of it is blubber anyhow. Unless, of course, you're a connoisseur of baby back ribs. Although, I'd personally recommend a good chianti with those.

Anyhow, when you're a deity like Anu, you can get away with murder. Remember the Great Flood? With one sweep, the Almighty annihilated everyone who was sinful, so—everyone. Everyone except Noah, that is, who either was very loyal or *very* good in bed. But when you're poor and hungry like Albert Fish, you eat one baby, and bam—you're locked up and electrocuted, cutting off power in Ossining for a week. What a waste of electricity. People in Ossining are mad and still waiting for a refund from Con Edison. A "con" indeed.

Ashlyn

I hate it when parents take two different names like Ash and Lynn and amalgamate them into a single entity like Ashlyn in an attempt to make it sound unique. What a bore. Look, when Amazon took over and purchased Whole Foods, it didn't go all Amazoods.

Compiling several names together—like Susie and Anne into Suzanne, or Anna and Belle into Annabelle, or C and

Her into Cher—is not parenting; you're just playing with Legos.

Name-stacking is occasionally appropriate, though, such as when you want two or more children but you're only allowed one, as was during China's one-child policy (1979 to 2015). Other times, name-stacking is similar to binge-watching TV shows, overpacking for a vacation, and eating unlimited breadsticks at Olive Garden—greedy, greedy, greedy. As a parent, you'll simply look like an asshole with commitment issues who's unable to pick a single name and stick to it. Can't make decisions? Then put on a condom.

Bibi

Is it me, or does the name Bibi sound immoderately like "Beep, beep"? Honking is annoying! I hate it when drivers honk, especially by a road sign that in huge, bold letters caterwauls NO HONKING UNLESS FOR DANGER. I once witnessed an impatient schlepper in a MINI Cooper blasting his horn at a sweet little old lady. What's *dangerous* about her? Just because she's talking to herself, has a teardrop tattoo, and is carrying a massive hatchet, doesn't mean she's on a killing spree. Maybe there was a sale on hatchets, and I too love a good deal. But if you're still scared of her—don't fucking honk. Quietly run her over.

I can't take my friend Bibi anywhere. Whenever somebody calls her name, I automatically jump to the side, afraid I'll get hit by an upcoming car. If you want to name your children after sounds, sure go ahead, but why stop at Bibi? What's wrong with Woooosh, Chuchu, Vroomvroom, Brrrrrrrrrr, Meow, Woofwoof, Ticktock, Cock-a-doodle-do, or Nom-Nom-Nom-Nom-Nom? The final name on the list sounds outlandish, but at bare minimum it will remind you of the movie *Jaws: The Revenge*. Whenever you visit Fire Island or the Jersey Shore with Nom-Nom-Nom-Nom-Nom, you will keep imagining sharks and stay off the ocean where sea creatures can perforate you to death.

By the way, I hate *Jaws: The Revenge*. I find nothing fascinating about watching a toothy fish hunting rich white palookas. Unlike people who drive high, sharks aren't imbeciles, and they won't seek "revenge" by following a flock of flesh to the Bahamas—too long a journey for a feast. When sharks are hungry, they simply go to an all-you-can-eat buffet in Miami Beach.

For some reason, I always thought *Jaws: The Revenge* was about the contestants of *The Biggest Loser*, and how after the finale they go dining at Outback Steakhouse and order every item on the menu.

Billy
(or Hilly, Milly, Tilly, Willy...)

These names sound childish because they rhyme and culminate with a Y, visually reminding me of an orgy scene from the movie *Caligula*, which looked quite chaotic:

> Billy with his red chili looked dumb and silly bamboozling Hilly. Milly, who's ugly, really, arrived from Philly, and was getting chilly. While Tilly, whose voice is shrilly, resembled a filly, and she jumped on Willy...

Do you see how unintelligent that sounded? Adults should always be Bill, Hill, Mill, Till, and Will. Except I also want to denounce the name Will because of my ex.

Will was a tree conservationist who broke up with me upon learning how much toilet paper I go through caring for my moneymaker, and that breakup left me unreasonably bitter. To this day, I hate all the forest constituents such as grass, flowers, bushes, and trees. And whenever I go hiking, I don't wait until the nearest rest stop. I shamelessly take a dump straight in the woods.

Brie

Let's see if I get this straight. Somehow Brie, after cheese, is an appropriate name for a child, but Mozzarella, Manchego, or Schloss is not?

Brie doesn't even look appetizing—a white, crusty-ass one-year-old wheel. If I wanted to see something white and crusty I can visit my cousin Vlad. Yet Brie is often described as sumptuous, delicate, or "enhanced with jam." The truth is, brie is so damn stinky that whenever they say it's "enhanced with jam," I say it's "camouflaged with jam." Then they have the audacity to bake it, after which the room smells like a hot yoga studio. And you thought microwaving fish was bad.

I have a friend Brie who is such a worldly cunt. She is a chef—with an ego bigger than her nostrils—and because she is so good at what she does, she thinks she is better than everyone else and has this smirky grimace on her face that makes her look cuntstipated. Look, I am all about empowering others, but don't get too cocky and cuntfident as to tell me one day you will find a way to cure cancer. Yes, she did! The only thing Brie is capable of curing is a hind leg of a pig to make prosciutto. Add some bread, some Brie, and you've got yourself a charcuterie board. If it sounds like I'm venting is because I am, as I haven't talked to my therapist in two weeks. And speaking of venting, I need to turn on the vent and aerate my room, as this Brie conversation has stunk up the whole damn place.

If you must name your bundle of joy after items found primarily at the grocery store, try something more palatable such as Olive, Rosemary, or Clementine. Beautiful names, sure. Just don't be surprised when you only see your dear Clementine from October through January when she's in season. While your Rosemary may be stuffed into a turkey's ass, and Olive will be swimming in a dirty martini . . . Anyhow, if I had a point, I lost it.

Britney

What does Britney have in common with Whitney, Titney, Fortney, and Courtney?

They all end with *ney*, which sounds exactly like *nay*, which means *no*. Why so negative? I come from a long line of optimists, where instead of saying "No," we say, "Not a yes."

Once after a "less than perfect" first date, the guy asked me on a second date, and I rejected him with, "My calendar is already full, but if something opens up, I'll give you a call."

Now compare Britney to Yesmine. With Yesmine, especially if she doesn't speak English, you'll never hear, "No." What I'm trying to say is that if anal or blowjobs are essential to you, don't date a Britney and find yourself a Yessica or at least a Maybeca.

The only Britney that doesn't annoy me is Britney Spears. I'm all about #FreeBritneyBitch, and I'm pumped that her conservatorship (also known as "prison") ended. But don't you think Britney's story is just like the movie *Aladdin*? Princess Jasmine—who has everything, lives in a palace, yet wants to get out—is not unlike Britney Spears and her conservatorship. Only, Princess Jasmine has a big, angry puss who defends her; but Britney's attorney is not that scary-looking. What I hate is that both stories end well, which is a shame. I would have loved seeing Princess Jasmine marrying Jafar, becoming obsessed with Chardonnay, and starring in *The Real Housewives of Agrabah*. Not just *Aladdin,* ALL Disney movies are based on real life, according to my Wikipedia research.

Cinderella—an OCD freak who is delusional, who talks to animals, crashes parties, loses shoes and other shit all over the place, yet somehow manages to snatch a handsome man—is that about me?

Finding Nemo—a story about a dumb orange fish who is so dumb that he gets himself in all sorts of dumb problems—Donald Trump.

Lady and the Tramp—two characters date, eat spaghetti, deal with so much drama; the guy is an ugly dog, yet very charismatic and a womanizer; the woman is gorgeous but ends up having four of his kids—Ye and Kim K much?

WALL•E—a gang of cranky people on a long flight, strapped to their seats, and served by loyal robots . . . One day you'll understand when you take a plane to India.

Brooklyn

Brooklyn is not a person I hate but a part of New York City that's just "too far": It's too far from Central Park, too far from Tiffany's, and even too far from the sun. Yes, every time I'm in a sketchy neighborhood such as Bed-Stuy or Ozone Park, I'm Vitamin-D-and-wallet-deficient.

Why do people who live in downtown Brooklyn invite you to visit? I have enough snooty people and overpriced bagels in my own neighborhood. At least ours are fresh.

Brooklyn is obsessed with camouflaging genitalia into their neighborhood names, such as Bushwick, Canarsie, or Gowanus. There's also the smelly Barftown, but for some reason they call it Brighton Beach.

What I hate the most about Brooklyn is the Brooklyn Bridge. It's loooooong and it's booooooooring. If I wanted something long and boring, I'd start reading *War and Peace*.

Cedric to Donald

Cedric
Cesar
Charley
Christina

Claude
Clint
Crystal
Curtis
Dan
David
Delia
Dick
Divanna
Don
Donald

Cedric

The name Cedric sounds like somebody took the words cedar, cider, and sick—tumbled them in a drier—and voila. This is precisely why Cedric is not a name but a combination of three dry, warm words that smell like Downy.

Now I'm cranky and riled up because I detest folding laundry, the most annoying chore. Roomba will sweep your floor, the dishwasher will clean your dishes, but nobody will fold your laundry for you—unless you drop it off at a laundromat. Luckily, I'm not in the business of paying extra for another human being touching my delicates or folding my T-shirts into pinwheels the way Marie Kondo does. Listen, if I wanted to learn how to fold like the Japanese, I would simply implement an attack on Pearl Harbor and see what happens.

I hate companies that sell laundry products. Like why does Arm & Hammer—the company that sells baking soda—sell detergents? Did people stop baking all of a sudden? By the way, whenever I hear "Arm & Hammer," I immediately envision Ted Bundy on a killing spree.

Procter & Gamble should stop wasting their time on cleaning products, change their name, and move to Vegas with a slogan: "Gamble & Gamble & Keep on Gambling. Then you'll understand why we're in the 'cleaning' business."

And Tide promises ninety-three loads. So does a weekend on Fire Island.

What about "imaginative" laundry scents such as Clean and Fresh, Spring Meadow, or Mountain Breeze? Remember the last time you hiked up a mountain in the summer, felt the breeze, and swatted millions of mosquitos along the way? That's exactly what the scent smells like. They should write on the bottle: "With our new scent called Mountain Breeze, and the new formula full of dyes, nitrates, and sulfites, you'll itch all over the place, you dumbass."

As a society, we are forced into "cleanliness" by the aforementioned companies because it's a multi-trillion-dollar business. So when we stop buying cleaning products, profits plummet. That's why laundry commercials portray stinky children and a voice on the background that gives you a visual: "With our detergent, your dirty children will smell like Serena Williams after a match—smelling fresh!"

To sum up: I HATE DOING LAUNDRY.

Cesar

My friend Cesar is one of those annoying people who only talk about saving the planet. He says the levels of CO2 are rising, causing global warming, and the burning of fossil fuels, such as driving to work, is the main culprit. The double whammy here is that the Amazon rainforest is thinning out, and trees are vital because they suck on CO2, release oxygen, blah, blah, and blah. That's why I don't see Cesar very often.

To save the planet, Cesar drinks seltzer by the gallon, which is basically water with CO2. He figures the more he drinks, the less CO2 will be released into the atmosphere.

CO2 this, CO2 that . . . Calm the fuck down! The Earth has survived five ice ages, multiple asteroids, fires, tsunamis, earthquakes, ISIS, pirates, and sweatpants in public.

I say, Cesar, if you want to save the planet, then go save it. The Amazon rainforest isn't going to suddenly reappear just because you're thirsty. Instead of reaching for a bottle of seltzer, why not grab a sickle and begin murdering truck drivers who are responsible for all that CO2? Sure, massacres are illegal, but you gotta start somewhere. Glaciers in Antarctica won't stop melting just because you're unwilling to get your hands dirty.

I don't know about you, but global warming sounds like a perfect solution for everything. I love the idea of sunny weather and mojitos all year round. You don't even have to travel to places like Florida or Hawaii for a tan, when you can do it straight from your backyard in Yonkers. Inadvertently, world-traveling will diminish, and CO2 levels will drop, causing global cooling. The advantage of this plan is that *our* generation gets to enjoy the warmer climate and drinks by the pool. Who cares about the next generation? Plus, once the glaciers melt, the pool will be everywhere. I simply can't wait to jump out of the window onto something inflatable and paddle to work.

Charley

I despise the name Charley because it reminds me of charley horses. In case you're unaware, a charley horse is a muscle spasm in the leg that is short-lived like Trump's presidency, but which hurts like a motherfucker like Kristen Stewart's acting. I'm a runner, so I get charley horses more than Charley Sheen gets herpes.

By the way, I have a hard time understanding what muscle spasms have to do with horses. Do muscle spasms smell, live in a stall, or play for the Denver Broncos? Most importantly, if you have equinophobia (or fear of horses), would you still get charley horses? It's all very confusing.

However, if you think outside the box, you can always find a silver lining in a charley horse. Next time a stallion starts galloping inside your calf muscle, just contact the Kentucky Derby and sign your charley horse up for a race. The 2024 Derby "purse"—the amount of money the racers will share—is five million dollars. Even if you don't snatch the first prize of $1.86 million, at least you'll see Kentucky, where you'll understand why Senator Mitch McConnell always looks like the frown emoji. You'll land in Louisville and realize everyone looks the same. You'll think, *Wow, is that because they're all cousins or because they're all white?* Then you'll realize, *Oh, right. They're all inbred.*

Fun fact: in Wilbur, Washington, there's a $300 fine for riding an "ugly" horse. So when Honey Boo Boo cantered through Wilbur, she was fined twice: once for being ugly and once for eating grass off a private property. No worries, all good. She recouped the money by coming in second at the Equine Cup. Adam Driver came first.

Christina

Chris, Christian, and Christina sound too much like "Christ," like not even subtle. Such plagiarism is not okay with me. Conceal, but don't steal. Rearrange some letters or something. I see no reason why Chris can't be Sirch or why Christina can't be Aiichrstn.

The real reason why I hate names that sound "Christey" is because of the misogyny.

See, when Eve—a woman—got a teensy bit hungry and ate an apple for lunch, she got kicked out of Eden with nothing but a leaf over her beaver. A hungry, naked woman running around by herself? That screams disaster.

But when Jesus Christ—a man—turned water into wine, none of his friends complained, even if the wine was a bottom shelf Pinot Grigio. Free is free. They got loose on the booze, then they schmoozed and sang blues.

Plus, Christ had an entire *supper* catered in his honor, during which he sat in front of da Vinci for a portrait, stuffing his greedy face. But if Eve had been living in Jesus's time, do you think she would have been invited to a significant dinner party like that?

The question is, would *you* want to invite Eve—starved and unclothed—to an important event where you must wear a suit and a tie? I mean I wouldn't. But that's not the point. Women, in general, must work harder in order to be recognized. For example, Frida Kahlo spent years painstakingly sitting in front of the mirror getting hemorrhoids and learning brushstrokes just so she could eventually share with the world her gift: her mustache and the caterpillar above her eyes. But Abraham Lincoln? Because he was a man and the president, all he had to do was Frida ~~Kahlo~~ slaves, and ta-da—now his mug is printed on anything round and copper.

In the Bible especially, misogyny is everywhere. For example, turn to 1 Cor. 11:3 and you will find: "Christ is the head of every man, and the husband is the head of his wife." If you are visualizing a man's face on a woman's body that would simply look like Victoria Beckham.

And what about Noah (a man), and how he lured every animal into his Arc to prevent a mass extinction and became a hero, while Eve (a woman) ran around forest au naturel and shoeless and became the first woman to get athlete's foot.

By the way, it's a little unbelievable that there were so many animal couples on the Arc without a single divorce and only one interbreeding (when Noah screwed an angry, disagreeable mule. That's how we have Simon Cowell).

Claude

I loathe that good-for-nothing narcissist, Claude Monet. Have you seen his impressionist work? Water Lilies is a series of 250 paintings, and all of them are blurry or out of focus. For an impressionist, I'm not impressed.

I don't know about you, but I could draw perfect landscapes in second grade. My art teacher thought my work was from the Renaissance after I'd started drawing women in the nude. There was nothing blurry about my work. In fact, the resolution of some of the body parts was so sharp you could cut your fingers on them.

But Monet—a professional artist—couldn't be bothered to add a few extra strokes. I'd understand if Claude Monet suffered from hyperopia (when you see fuzzy up-close), yet there's not a single photo of him wearing glasses. You could argue that because of his cataracts, his vision was compromised, but again, that's not an excuse if your work costs a fortune. He charges twenty million dollars for one ancient painting, yet he's too lazy to drop by Warby Parker for a pair of bifocals. Do you know who refuses to wear glasses? An egomaniac. So I'm done with Monet and his blurry Water Lilies. Now, the only time I want to see anything blurry is when it's Cinco de Mayo, and I'm on my seventh margarita.

Clint

The name CLINT frosted on a birthday cake always looks like CUNT. There's almost no space between the L and the I, and even the most powerful cake decorator, with the steadiest hand, will mess it up.

While volunteering for Hillary Clinton's campaign in 2019, I was in charge of ordering a cake for an important milestone. It was my luck that the pastry chef wrote TRUMP instead of CUNT ON. Phew—I was saved.

I once worked at a restaurant, and Clint was one of the waiters. He was dumber than a blueberry muffin and probably got the job based solely on his looks. The interview must have gone something like, "Clint, did you graduate high school?"

"No."

"You're hired."

He was pretty but annoying—so pretty annoying—and he always asked for favors. Every time he needed his shift covered, he'd say, "You scratch my back, Jeremy, and I'll scratch yours." Finally I said, "No, hoe. If you scratch my back without my consent, I'm using my Taekwondo and feng shui skills and kicking your ass." Then I got him a cake for his birthday—HAPPY BIRTHDAY, CUNT. Everyone agreed.

Crystal

If you can't afford Swarovski but still want some crystals in your home, avoid naming your baby Crystal, and here's why. Indian, Chinese, and Brazilian children that mine minerals to make ends meet—it's called child labor—don't benefit whatsoever if you fail to purchase their products—gemstones and whatnot. These children wake up at the crack of dawn, attend the mining university to learn the craft, and spend the rest of their long but miserable lives digging tunnels and mining jewels just so people like you could have something sparkly on their extending pinkies while they slurp on dirty martinis. These child wonders—workaholics—hone their skills over decades, which is the reason why crystals are so darn expensive.

To compare, if you give birth to a baby and call her Crystal, relatively no skills are needed. I mean, schtupping without a condom doesn't require a degree. And unlike high-end jewelry, if kids were unaffordable to have, somebody would have caught on centuries ago and put an end to it. Yet we're still procreating, and there are eight billion of us. But there's only one of each: the Black Orlov Diamond, the Dresden Green, and the Graff Pink. The lesson here is that you should support your local child-owned businesses. Of course, it's illegal and environmentally damaging, but at least the kids will know they don't wake up for nothing.

Curtis

Curtis? What kind of name is Curtis? Curtis sounds a lot like *cortis*, which is short for cortisol, which is the body's primary stress hormone. Too much cortisol leads to weight gain, trouble sleeping, and depression. And I have a friend, Curtis, who's driving me bonkers!

No wonder my cortisol levels are high, I'm gaining weight, and my anxiety is through the roof. Curtis bitches about everything, be it a price increase on Prada shirts or his leaky gut.

Enough with the complaining, Curtis! Can't afford Prada? Try T.J. Maxx. Sure, they only have one size—X Ugly—but at least you'll save some money for antidepressants and will finally stop complaining about your damn leaky gut.

Dan

Dan, my friend from college, is one of those health nuts who can't stop talking about nutrition. He's the picture of health and, like a picture, he's hung—or so you could tell whenever he wears grey sweatpants. He's from Florida and his parents must have been anteaters, because, aside from him being slow and cute, Dan's got the biggest tongue I've ever seen. To accessorize his best feature, he pierced his tongue with a stud, so whenever he opens his mouth, it's like staring at an anteater with a pierced tongue. And I can't stand animal abuse!

Anyhow, the other day, Dan told me I should be eating more fiber after witnessing me ordering a burger at a restaurant. First of all, chill the fuck out. Just because I ordered a burger it doesn't mean I eat like that all the time. I was intoxicated, and the best way to eliminate beer breath is by masticating something succulent and beefy.

I turned to Dan. "Why do I need fiber?"

Dan said, "Fiber is not actually for you, but for the friendly bacteria in your gut."

I asked, "Why the fuck would I feed bacteria instead of myself? That's very illogical. Besides, the gut bacteria can't be that friendly, considering they've never stopped by to introduce themselves or done anything for me. They live rent-free in my belly, don't pay any utilities, don't help with chores, and yet find the time to complain about the lack of fiber. As long as those privileged bitches live under Daddy's roof, they play by my rules."

So I smacked my belly and told the bugs living inside, "No more complaining, you needy dimwits. Irregardless* whether I chomp on some bull testicles in Spain after *la corrida de toros* or share a cricket or two with Bear Grylls in the wilderness of Montana. If you need fiber that desperately, then go get a fucking job!"

* By the way, "irregardless" is a word. It means "regardless" and according to Merriam-Webster—my loyal bitch—while the word is nonstandard, it's been used for well over 200 years. That means "irregardless" has existed longer than the car, the light bulb, and the periodic table of elements. "Irregardless" has survived World War I and II and—together with Elon Musk and other rich billionaires—"irregardless" will survive World War III because they'll escape to Mars. So, grammar lunatics, get over yourselves and get a life. And if I get a negative review from you on Amazon because you disagree, I'll track your ass down and plow you to the ground. Y'all've been warned.

David

The name David has five letters, and five is the ultimate number. There are five fingers on each hand, five boroughs in Manhattan, and five cells in Kanye West's brain. David is the most perfect name. That's precisely why I hate it.

My friend David is a wealthy wine connoisseur and has over 500 bottles stored in his cellar. But how is it fair that when David drinks two bottles of wine, he's a connoisseur, but when I do the same, I'm called an alcoholic.* *David* is the one with an entire cellar; I'm just a broke amateur!

I hate regular math, but I looooove alcohol math, which is when you count how many calories you've consumed while drinking. So 500 bottles at around 625 calories per bottle comes down to 312,500 calories. No wonder David's put on weight and has obtained an hourglass figure. More like an hour and a half. No wonder the rotund bastard is always late.

* Btw, "alcoholic" is an outdated, discriminatory term similar to "retard," and I prefer a more upbeat, modern term "ethanol enthusiast." If you insist on shaming people for abusing liquid with 13% alcohol content, be my guest to 1) go to hell, and 2) come back from hell, and then go back to hell. So you could become the first idiot who died twice from not drinking.

Delia

My friend Delia is one of those skinny vegans who's all about recycling and biking to work to "save the planet." She's so vegan, even vegans hate her. The ironic part is that Delia loves flying long distances to places like India or the moon, completely oblivious that jet fuel releases greenhouse gasses that cause temperatures to rise, *destroying* the planet. Plus, after prolonged sun damage with her excessive biking, Delia's vegan skin is all dark and leathery and reminds me of fried chicken. Talk about irony.

By the way, have you noticed that bike lanes are painted green? What's green about them? It's not like all these bikers are pedaling around and planting trees or drinking jet fuel so less of it is released into the stratosphere.

Compare that to a true ecologist, Ted Bundy. He murdered 200-plus carnivores, which reduced cow farts by a solid 37 percent. Plus, with 200 fewer cars on the streets of LA, during his reign of terror, the pollution dropped to a record low, and you could finally breathe and see the ocean in the distance.

Dick

I hate diminutives, in general—but Dick for Richard? Where's the family resemblance? Dick looks adopted, and from the look of things, he's not even in the will.

I can kind of see Fanny in Frances and Terry in Terence, but where's Peggy in Margaret? Unless she's gotten pegged in the fanny while drinking a marg, I don't see it.

If you shorten a name, make sure it sounds similar to the original. Like Barb for Barbara, Josh for Joshua, and Prolapse Mouth for Donatella Versace.

Divanna

My friend Divanna is a conspiracy theorist and says we haven't landed on the moon. She's so annoying. Who *doesn't* know that? How can you possibly touch down on something round like the moon? That's why we have no problems landing on Earth because our planet is flat.

Divanna says Bigfoot is real. Duh, we've all seen Shaquille O'Neal with his size 23 feet.

Divanna also believes Amelia Earhart was captured and killed by the Japanese. That's a great theory, but here's the problem: First of all, the Japanese couldn't have captured her. Have you tried seizing a plane lately? It's kind of hard. Even with a strong netting designed for whales, you still have to be at least 3,000 feet tall to reach the sky, and the median height in Japan is four feet, nine inches. And second, Amelia is from Atchison, Kansas. I think she actually escaped her miserable hometown by moving to Japan. Amelia was way better off, even if that led to her death. I mean, Japanese cuisine is to die for.

Don

The reason why I hate Don is that Don sounds too much like *dong*, and I don't like names that are synonymous with "penis"; and yes, Dick and Willy, you're also in that category.

Similarly, I've met Pusina and Kanti, and I couldn't bring myself to say either name out loud. I abhor a plethora of things in life, but funny words/names aren't one of them.

The C-word and the N-word are my favorite, and they are codswallop and nincompoop.*

My hot tip? Don't give your baby a "penacious" name like Don, or a "vaginacious" name like Pusina for the same reason you don't take candy from strangers or walk alone at night in a dark neighborhood—it's downright stupid. I mean, while it sounds fun, do you really wanna risk your life and eat that candy with who-knows-how-many calories and sugar?

* Codswallop and nincompoop, respectively, mean *mad* and *stupid*. So . . . Don Quixote de la Mancha.

Since none of you read, as you're all idiots, Don Quixote de la Mancha is a character from a boring novel by a delirious writer Miguel de Cervantes called *Don Quixote*. So this character, Don, is a middle-aged man—named after Miguel's penis—who decides to become a knight. First of all, who the fuck decides to become a knight? In the book, Don Quixote is snollygoster and flibbertigibbet (*shrewd* and *flakey*).

By wanting to become a knight, Don was obviously going through a midlife crisis, but how is riding a horse with a giant lance a fun activity when you're over fifty? Your nuts are now crushed, and your legs resemble a wheelbarrow. If you simply need to deform yourself, ask Jocelyn Wildenstein for the name of her plastic surgeon.

Donald

When I hear the name Donald, I immediately get angry—angrier than a real housewife without a bottle of Chardonnay in the fridge. The most annoying Donald of them all? Donald Duck.

If Donald Duck was anthropomorphic—meaning he was not only a cartoon character but also had human attributes—then why couldn't he wear some pants like humans do? Or a dress? Maybe a pair of boxers? Even a thong would suffice.

When an extra-large American bullfrog, Donald Trump, rallied across the states, he had the decency to smear some orange paint on his face in an ill-fated attempt to blend in. He even acted like a human.

If Donald Duck simply lounged at home, it wouldn't bother me. But he was on national TV, and kids were watching.

Look, when you're in Alaska, do what Alaskans do: Go hunting, vote Republican, and hook up with a moose. But when you're on national TV or on a Zoom call—cover your pussy up.

Elizabeth
to
Ivy

Elizabeth
Elle
Emily
Eric
Eve
Ezequiel
Felicia
Felicity
Florina
Franzy
Frida

George
Georgia
Gian
Henok
Hudson
Hung
India
Ivy

Elizabeth

Elizabeth is a loooooooooooong name. Which, in my opinion, is veryyyyyyyyy narcissistic. Out of Elizabeth, you could easily construct Eliza, Beth, Ethel, and many more. But out of Nusa, a Hungarian name? All you get is *Anus*.

Plus, have you been to Elizabeth, NJ? If the traffic doesn't kill you, the smell will. The only reason Elizabeth has a population of 130,000 is because you need to pay a toll to get out. People say, "But, look, Elizabeth can't be all that bad because the great Judy Blume is from there!" Exactly. That's why she paid the toll and moved to Key West.

Plus, there's an IKEA in Elizabeth, and as a former IKEA employee, I can decidedly assure you that if you go there "just to look," you'll end up spending no less than two hundred bucks on deceivingly cheap paraphernalia that will be pouring over your shopping cart. What's more, my manager's name at IKEA was also Elizabeth. That's a lie. Her actual name was Dragon Breath Cooper (or D.B. Cooper). She hated me for no reason, and one time when I took longer than the allotted thirty minutes for lunch she was up in my face.

"Jeremy," she barked, "you're four minutes and twenty seconds late! This is unacceptable!"

In my head I told her, "So what, D.B. Cooper? It's like saying the sky is blue or that you smell like a tampon—it's obvious. Tell me something I don't know, like the amount of time passed since you last trimmed your eyebrows. They're waaaaay out-of-control, girl. In fact, they're so long and uneven, there's a bush outside that looks neater, plus it can grow forsythia. The only thing yours can grow is people's beliefs that you actually *are* the real Chewbacca."

She opened her vent again, "This is your last warning!"

In my head I replied, "You need to learn the definition of the word 'last' as this is the third time you've used it. 'Last' means 'terminal', not unlike your stupidity for which there's no cure."

Instead, the polite person I am, I emitted, "I apologize, and I promise that next time I'll be on time."

Then later I went downstairs to the parking garage and keyed her Nissan Cube. The moral of the story is: food is to be ravished, not rushed, as after all I'm not a ferocious beast who swallows faster than a sumo wrestler at a hotdog eating contest or Laura Spelman on her knees before John

Rockefeller, her sugar daddy. I have manners, people. True, I'm a shady bitch, but when I'm having lunch I'm like Kate Middleton—a fucking lady!

Elle

Elle is a palindrome—a word that reads the same backward as forward. Other palindromes are Anna, Bob, and Hannah. I hate them all because I find it unfair that Jeremy backward is Ymerej, which either sounds like a harsh industrial cleaner or a pretentious resort in Dubai. And what about LANA in reverse? Take your time...

These palindrome names—Elle, Anna, and Bob—reek of narcissism. Like salt, sulfites, nitrates, Red 40, refined carbohydrates, trans fats, and high-fructose corn syrup—THEY HAVE INFILTRATED EVERYTHING:

> ELLEr, intELLEctual, mademoiSELLE.
> ANNAl, wANNAbee, hosANNA.
> BOBcat, skiBOBbing, keBOB.

How greedy, selfish, arrogant, egotistical, self-centered, vainglorious, supercilious is that? Just a grotesque display of self-absorption. And don't even get me started on those inane palindrome phrases that read the same backward as forward: "I did, did I?" or "Was it a cat I saw?" or "Eva, can I see bees in a cave?"

Look, if you don't know whether you did or didn't do something, what a cat looks like, and that bees don't live in a cave, then you're either: one— stupid, or two—your name is Elle, Anna, or Bob (or most likely three— you're both).

Emily

So . . . this story is impossibly dark, but trust me, it's worth it. Emily, from Latin "Aemilia," means "eager," which means "needy," which—in my book (like, literally in *this* book)— means "narcissistic," and I hate narcissism. One of the few "isms" that I tolerate is necrophilism, which is when someone invites a very cold-hearted person to "Netflix and chill."

After I die, for instance, I'd love to get laid at least once for the road, and sure, I may not feel a thing but I'm a giver through and through. Besides, who knows what lies ahead after you're buried? Do you get laid in the afterlife and, more important, is there an afterlife to begin with? Are there sex toys? What kind?

Dead people are cold and blue, not unlike the blue whale in the Atlantic. You're dead, cold, and look like a whale and someone STILL finds you attractive. Be fucking grateful! You've never even gotten that much traction when you were alive.

Another "ism" that I stand behind is cannibalism, which is when someone loves eating hummus, I mean humans. I don't know about you, but after I pack my shit to move in with God, I'd rather be eaten by somebody I trust, like my cat or my creepy neighbor, than an agglomeration of ravenous worms in cold soil. Depending on how much you weigh, you could provide food for weeks for a family of five. Some of you may be disgusted by the thought of eating people, but you eat carcasses all the time, like dead pigs and dead cows. You even eat dead chicken fetuses, and that's only breakfast. Go ahead and grimace all you want.

Sure, consent is important in both instances, which is why I tattooed EAT ME above my butthole—in six languages. I'm sure necrophiles and cannibals in most countries will know what to do. Bon appétit.

>	Mange moi
>	Borða mig
>	Cómeme
>	Съешь меня
>	Eat Me
>	Мені же

Eric

My friend Eric refers to his anus as a "crack," and I hate it when people use metaphors excessively. Have you ever seen a crack, like the one in a wall? Cracks are minor, like Ghislaine Maxwell's sexual partners. But if your anus has met a penile object, it's no longer a crack, it's the Great Canyon.

Look, metaphors are only appropriate when what you're trying to convey will sound inappropriate. For instance, in a classroom setting, it is preferred to say "cameltoe" instead of "jammed vagina," and it is also preferred to say "butterface" instead of "yellow-just-like-butter-but-it's-really-from-jaundice face." "Aunt Flow" means "menstruation," and "Uncle Sam" means the "U.S. government." Marry Aunt Flow and Uncle Sam together and you've got yourself the Grand Old Party.

In summation: If you must use metaphors, at least know what they mean. So if you have "tunnel vision," get out of the fucking tunnel and stop complaining, and if you see the "light at the end of the tunnel," congratulations, you're not dying. You've simply made it through the Lincoln Tunnel—welcome to New Jersey, buttmunch.

Eve

Eve was Adam's wife, the second lady of humanity, and animal abuser. If you don't believe me, look up her pictures online. On every one of them, she's wrapped in a huge anaconda, which, thankfully, later poisoned her lunch, yet Justin Bieber can't buy exotic Savannah cats without backlash.

According to some religious accounts, Eve's occupation was "co-manager of God's creation." How did she become a manager so quickly without a high school diploma—plus no skills or clothes? Listen, even my local McDonald's requires their workers to at least wear shoes.

Look, the whole story of Adam and Eve is suspicious. Eve had given birth to six children, yet in every picture her underwear is this one slutty-looking, teensy-weensy leaf. Nobody can be that tight after giving birth to six children, not even with a good plastic surgeon performing vagina rejuvenation. Ask Octomom. Her vagina doubles as a water slide at DreamWorks Water Park in Rutherford, NJ (and in wintertime, it's a perfect slope for snowboarding).

My theory is that Eve was vain and egotistical and when Adam would fall asleep, she'd harvest his ribs—the same ribs that had magically created her—and the ribs would turn into children. Unfortunately, ribs don't grow back, and Adam kept getting thinner and thinner. But instead of suspecting Eve, he just figured his keto diet was finally working.

Ezequiel

If you say "Ezequiel" with a French accent, it sounds like "a sequel," and sequels are the bane of my existence. Spoilers, am I right?

Batman Returns? Talk about a spoiler! Now I know that Batman doesn't bite the dust in the first flick. If nobody dies, is it even an action movie? Bernie Madoff probably got more action in the prison shower than Batman does in his cinematic career.

And what about those colon-titled movies? *Spider-Man: Far from Home*. That colon screams "SEQUEL!" So if Spider-Man is far from home, that means he (Tom Holland, in this case) is ashamed of his old digs in the first movie—maybe a bedbug infestation, a multitude of cats, or a mountain of dirty dishes drove him out—so he ran away from home. I have zero interest in going to the Multiplex where I'll spend $15 to sit in a filthy chair and eat stale popcorn while watching a movie about sloppy mess—when I could simply just stay at home, gobble on Hawaiian pizza, and watch a few episodes of *Hoarders* without leaving the couch.

Then there are the numbered atrocities. *How to Train Your Dragon 2*. Dude, how long does it take to train a fucking dragon?

If my life were a series of cinematic masterpieces, here are the sequels:

Jeremy Returns. He goes back to the mall to return every impulse purchase. The salesclerk gives him the side-eye, like "I knew you couldn't afford this, you broke bitch!"

Jeremy: Far from Home. He announces he's moving from New York to New Jersey, and everyone runs away from him like he's King Kong. But instead of climbing the Empire State Building, this classy lady takes the elevator.

How to Train Jeremy 2. They put him on a train at Penn Station and give him a one-way ticket to New Jersey. "Don't ever come back!" they warn. "There's no budget for the third installment!"

Felicia

Oh Felicia, Felicia, Felicia... No name is more synonymous with farewell than Felicia.

If you must say goodbye to anyone, say goodbye to Felicia, aka "Felicity" Huffman, whose character Lynette on *Desperate Housewives* is more annoying than a vegan on a juice cleanse. Lynette stocks up on Adderall but fails to share with anyone. Selfish bitch. Now compare Lynette to Harvey Weinstein's roommate at Wende Correctional Facility, who selflessly sacrificed his limited living space with a convicted sex offender. Now that's real love.

Speaking of love, I've been a giver for as long as I can remember. When I was nine, I was inspired by the *Watch Tower* magazine, grew a beard, and thought of myself as a reincarnated Jesus Christ. That's when I decided to start volunteering and donating food to those in need. I was nine, so I wasn't sure how to donate—except walking around and throwing eggs at cars. I figured if those people couldn't afford parking garages, they were probably hungry.

Felicity

Back to Felicity Huffman. First of all, I hate that her last name is Huffman and not Huffwoman. Besides, "huff" sounds like "half," and half & half is fattening.

Second of all, according to Merriam-Webster, to "huff" means to "utter," "to utter" means "to offer," and "to offer" means "to propose as payment." So "to huff" then means "to propose as payment." Does that somehow tie in with Huffman's college scandal, after which she went to Dublin, California, to serve eleven days in federal prison?

"To huff" also means "to make angry." But I wonder who's angrier, Felicity Huffman because she had to go to prison, or the woman she met there, who made Felicity her bitch and lovingly called her Felicity Huffmuffin. Like all true lesbian relationships, they moved in together the same day—can't help not to (I mean it's prison and all)—but unfortunately their romance had to end in less than two weeks. What a shame. But they still write to each other, I hope.

Florina

Florina is a hop, skip, and a Zoom call away from being miswritten as Florida, which is nothing but a state full of people with more dough stashed away than a bakery. All secured in safes.

By the way, have you tried lifting a safe? You can't because it's six hundred pounds. Multiply that by a trillion safes in Florida to understand why Florida is sinking from all that weight and tilting the rest of the states up. That's how people end up in Florida—they leave their homes and gravity pulls them downhill. My friend Rob went for an iced latte in Manhattan and tumbled down straight to Fort Lauderdale.

Why do people keep storing valuables in a safe? If I were rich, I'd wear so many diamonds, even muggers would not be able to carry them all. I would make flower arrangements out of $100 bills and give them away as party gifts to my poor friends—and like Jeff Bezos, I wouldn't pay income taxes, a handsome upside when you're rich! What I'm saying is:

Roses are red and violets are blue.
On the first date always ask, "How rich are you?"

Franzy

My manager Franzy is a self-proclaimed activist who always brings up climate change, dying animal breeds, or nutritional news.

Last month she said, "Did you know that toilet paper wipes out ninety-four acres of trees which contributes to global warming?"

I said, "Toilet paper doesn't wipe anything out. It just sits there on CVS shelves, bothering nobody. So what if a few trees suffer? At least my tushy is thriving. If places had been reversed, trust me, a tree would have cut you in half as well."

Another time Franzy started a conversation with, "Did you know humpback whales are dying?"

I asked, "Why, because you talked to them about toilet paper, and they got bored to death?"

Last week, as I sprayed palm oil on a pan, Franzy said, "Palm oil clogs arteries!"

I looked at my palm—then her face—and then the two of them met . . . at fifty miles per hour.

Frida

I hate names that sound like the word *free*, like Frida, Freesia, or Freelove.

"Free" is a seductive word. It promises something at no cost, but there's always an angle—unless you're pure and selfless to the core, like Mother Teresa or Luigi Mangione. Nothing in this world is truly free, and it all started a long time ago in Eden. Do you remember those free, succulent Honeycrisp apples Eve was trying to enjoy? They were poisoned, for fuck's sake. And it only got worse from there.

It's the same with names, as names have meanings . . . for the most part. But some don't. There's no meaning to Dasha, Masha, Sasha, Nasha, Russia, Natasha, Usher . . . or Luigi. They sound like they're straight out of some romantic comedy—like *Penny Dreadful*—when there's no plot, just airtime to fill. So, you keep slapping consonants onto *ASHA* until it's over.

Your parents named you—*you*—for a reason. If they named you Rich, you better start saving money, honey. If they named you Destinie, you better get comfortable with the stripper pole, girl. And if they named you Teresa, you better like the missionary "positionary."

Finally, if your parents named you Frida, it's because that's how much you cost them on the black market, you kidnapped, half-baked imbecile. Call the police and find your real parents. Just don't come crying to me if they're ugly and broke and were the ones who sold you in the first place.

George

Contrary to popular belief, George Washington's dentures were not solely made of wood. In fact, they were a mixture of wood, and teeth from humans, cows, horses and elephants, with a touch of copper, brass, and even silver. Whenever he smiled, it was like a miniature hardware store in his mouth. Once, a jeweler even mistook him for a walking jewelry box.

The reason I hate George Washington is because of the way he died.

The "official" story is that he died from a throat infection, but that's not what happened. History books won't teach you that George Washington died while eating Sally Fairfax's pussy. Three of his wooden teeth ignited because her pussy was on fire.

He burned to death.

Georgia

One—I hate it when parents name their babies after the state where they were conceived. That just tells me the parents never left the state of Georgia and trust me, honey, there are prettier states out there, like Georgia in Europe. For fifty cents you could get hair implants *and* a happy ending.

Two—Georgia is just... too sexual and suggestive. Imagine your child's future. High school boys will be saying all kinds of inappropriate things, like:

"Have you seen Georgia's peach?"

"Oh, yeah, she is very ripe."

"Dude, I'm not talking about her armpits."

"Then what, her lunch?"

See? Kids are jerks (and stupid).

Anyhow, I've heard of Georgias, Dakotas, and Tennessees, but no Wyomings, Idahos, and Louisianas.

Why not?

Wild boy? Name him Wyoming.

Is he pasty, dull, and looks like a potato? Idaho.

Does he stink? Louisiana.

Three—forget it. Sometimes two points are enough.

Gian

The name Gian doesn't roll off the tongue. Gian's parents, in a fit of automotive-inspired creativity, once cobbled together a vehicle from discarded muffler clamps and rusty hubcaps. They then decided to name their son in a similarly haphazard manner.

Their other children were Niamh, Xiomara, Saoirse, and Bjorn—clink, clink, clink, and another vehicular monstrosity rolled off the assembly line. Unlike a Tesla, none of these cars are electric and, from the sound of things, will never get on the road.

By the way, Gian is pronounced either way, be it with a hard G like in "gonad" or with a soft G like in "genital." So when you take the assembled "Gian" for a test drive, avoid touching the stick shift. As some people have reported, it may spontaneously combust or, worse, experience an unexpected and rather intimate mechanical malfunction.

My friend Gian once complained to me. He said, "I don't understand why I don't have a boyfriend. I am such a great conversationalist."

I said, "The secret to finding—and keeping—a relationship is not to be a great conversationalist, but to know when to shut the fuck up."

Henok

Henok—Ethiopian in origin—is a misspelled name, similar to Ivanka, Barron, and Tiffany. By the way, their real names are Neurotic, Annoying, and Clubfoot.

Henok is a variation of the name Enok, which must mean "enoki mushrooms." I mean, what other explanation there is? The saddest part is that Henok's parents realized their baby resembled a mushroom and they wanted to honor that, yet they failed to come up with something more clever. I hate it when parents add silent letters to a name to disguise its true meaning. If your baby looks like a mushroom, don't be embarrassed. And if you are, you have to work harder than just adding an *h* to the word *enoki* and calling it a day.

My friend Henok is such a gullible guy. When I asked him about the origin of his name, Henok told me it was because when his parents held him for the very first time, they thought he looked like a "fun guy."

I can just see it now. The nurse delivered the baby, but when the mom saw it, she gasped and said, "Excuse us, but we did not order a mushroom for lunch. We ordered a salad."

"No," said the nurse, "this is not your lunch. This is your baby."

"Our BABY? How can this be our baby? He looks funny."

The nurse said, "He does, but that's what makes him look special."

The mom said, "He does—like the *chef's* special. Would you be able to recommend a name for a fun guy like that?"

The nurse said, "A name for a fungi . . . How about Henok?"

So they had no choice but to call their son Henok, completely unaware that enoki mushrooms are more commonly known as *velvet shank*, a much prettier name. What an embarrassment.

If your child looks "mushroomous," forget boring names such as Henok, Portobella, or Oyster. Try something exciting and vivacious: Livid Entoloma, Destroying Angel, Sulfur Tuft, Shiitake, or Deadly Fibrecap. But if I were you, I would stay away from naming your baby Ivory Funnel, also known as Clitocybe Dealbata, a very toxic kind. From my experience, the last thing you want in your life is another toxic relationship.

Anyhow, on top of his "enoki-look-alikeness," my friend Henok's pores are so huge they resemble a morel, a kind of a spongy and cratery mushroom. In fact, when people see his face they sometimes confuse him for a Scrub Daddy. They automatically squirt some Dawn on his face and start doing their dishes.

Hudson

Hudson is a terrible name for a person, but a magnificent name for a river. Have you ever tried crossing the Hudson on a ferry from New York to New Jersey? It costs an arm and a leg. That's why New York is overrun with serial killers—they're constantly harvesting limbs just to afford the ferry fare to see the Garden State.

People, please, please, please don't name your children after nature or words you can find in the globe. It makes me feel like you've run out of imagination. Sure, you're busy being pregnant (and let's be honest bloated and enormous) and tired of hearing everyone coo about your "glow" and "cute baby bump" which, let's face it, is code for "Wow, is that double chin new? So you *do* look like your mother!"

Dear Expectant Parents, if you need a good name for your bebé, you've come to the right place! My book offers at least 111 names to avoid. That includes all "watery" names like Rain, Brook, and Canal Street, as well as "leafy" ones, like Leaf, Willow, and George H. Bush. But for some reason I like names Bear, Rock, and Sequoia. Only Sequoia's real name is Bob the Drag Queen, and he is seven feet tall in heels.

The reason I hate "naturous" names is because I hate how unoriginal they are. Close Google Maps and look up in the sky. There are astronomical terms that will make your baby stand out in school—original as hell—Compound Telescope, Black Hole, or Messier Object. Just don't be surprised if Messier will become a messy bitch.

Hung

Hung was a guy I once met at a sex shop in San Francisco. Hung started chatting me up in line, and I thought he was cute and—Harvey Weinstein agrees with me—would be very popular in prison.

He said, "Hi, I'm Hung."

I said, "Hi, I'm Jeremy."

He said, "No, I'm very Hung."

I said, "I heard you. I'm very Jeremy."

He said, "Read between the lines, Jeremy: I'm *Hung*."

I said, "Read between the *lines*? There's only one line in the word *hung*. And why do I have to read anything? I have three sex toys in one hand and a whip in another. How much reading do you think I'm gonna get done tonight?"

He said, "Bye, Felicia, you're stupid in my book."

I said, "What book?"

He said, "I don't know."

I said, "Well, I do. You'll be stupid in my book."

He said, "Why am I stupid?"

I said, "Because it's *my* book, and I can do whatever I want. Your name is gonna be Hung."

He said, "But my name is Don!"

I said, "You look more like a Don't—and I hate negativity—so in my book your name is Hung."

Isaac

I try not to hate people whose names start with the letter I. Why? Try to come up with at least one person whose name begins with the letter I. You can't because there aren't many. Well, you obviously know Isaac because of Isaac Newton, but three more exist: Isabel, Isobel, and Isabella. So to preserve an already dying breed—as I'm clearly a devoted preservationist who loves the biodiversity of the English language—I'll leave the "I"-named-people alone.

But first, let me bitch about that asshole, Isaac Newtown.

Isaac Newton discovered gravity, and I hate that gravity pulls my balls toward the floor where it's dusty. My scrotum is not a damn Swiffer. Look, I get it that science is important and whatnot, but do I really need to know everything about everything? If I hadn't learned about gravity, my life wouldn't have been that much different. For instance, before science and Isaac Newton, my life was easy, and I simply assumed that the reason my balls sagged and that I had a big nose and gassy stomach was because God was mad at me.

By the way, do you remember *how* Isaac discovered gravity? The Dumb-Dumb was sitting under a tree during harvest season, and an apple fell on his head. What did he think *would* happen? Without a proper helmet, I will not even visit upstate New York in October where apples fall from every possible direction.

The problem with the apple story is that Isaac was actually sitting under a maple tree. If someone dropped an apple, it was probably because someone had gone to Whole Foods and had climbed up the maple tree for lunch and threw an apple at Isaac Newton because he was, I don't know, ugly? Annoying? Stupid? Did I mention "ugly"?

Narcissistic to the core, Newton was SIR Isaac Newton, which meant he was into bondage, and his sexual partners referred to him as "Sir." As the warden of the Royal Mint, which produced British currency, Newton apparently executed forgers, AKA people who make counterfeit money.

He personally tracked them down in seedy bars and, with his knowledge of ropes, poppers, and other kinks, Isaac used BDSM to his advantage while catching crooks, and that's the reason why BDSM gets such a bad rep.

Drag shows get lousy rep because of him also. To catch even more forgers, Newton started performing at drag brunches because he had the best wigs, but also because day drinking is fun. Whoever stuck fake bills up his titties was executed on the spot.

Have you noticed the pattern here? He's a trickster, that one, and I dislike tricksters. I also dislike a horse-lookalike Senator Josh Hawley because unlike Newton, he discovered absolutely nothing except how to be a moron, but how does that benefit our society? As much as I hate gravity, at least sometimes it's useful, such as when the sun uses its invisible force to keep our planet in close proximity. The only thing buck-toothish Josh Hawley keeps in close proximity is hay for his lunch.

By the way, I've tried BDSM as well. But, unfortunately, after a kinky sex party involving ropes—as I tried to undo the Palomar Knot—I fell, hit my head on the floor, and almost broke my foot, and do you know why? All because of gravity. And who fucking *discovered* gravity, may I ask? Exactly: Sir Isaac Newton. So I haaaaaaaaaaaaate him.

Ivy

Why do parents name their children Ivy after a poisonous plant? Yet so far, nobody has dared to name their child Dionaea Muscipula or Symplocarpus Foetidus, which—in English from Latin—translates to Venus FlyTrap and Eastern Skunk Cabbage. If you want to be adventurous, I've discovered more "planty" names for your children: Nipple Fruit, Clitoria Ternatea, and The Boob Cactus.

My friend Ivy is ugly beautiful or *Bleh*utiful—like a Pekingese. In high school, she played both leads in *Beauty and the Beast*. Some call her a butterface, but she's more refined, fancier than butter. Like ghee. She thinks she's ugly from the neck down, but I also think from the neck up, but that's just me. Sadly, because of her looks, Ivy believes she's unlovable, and that she'll end up marrying herself. Ivy is the most two-faced person I know, so what if at her wedding one side of her face says "I do" and the other side says "I don't"? How embarrassing would that be? I understand you wanna do some hanky-panky with yourself, but why make it official? Plus, what if the right side of your face wants a divorce in three years, and how do you divide your assets? I know Ivy is dumb so I cut her some slack. One time, she asked me how many quarters were in a football game . . . Take your time.

Jeff to Lydia

Jeff
Jeremy
John
Jonathan
Kaitlin
Karl
Karen
Katie
Kenya
Kevin
Kris
LaToya
Laura
Leah
Leonardo
Lilly
Liza
Louis
Lydia

Jeff

Names like Jeff, Jeffrey, and Jefferson drive me crazy. These names differ only slightly, much like the installments of *Fifty Shades of Grey*, but the underlying premise remains the same: boring. Where's the authenticity in that? Where's the plot? Jeff Bezos? Boring. Jeff Fatt? Too fat. The only interesting Jeff I can think of is Jeffrey Dahmer. He killed seventeen men and even ate some of them—and got himself a show on Netflix. Though, unfortunately, only one season.

But my friend Jeff from Queens? No network would give him a show because nobody wants to waste their time on a show about a Jeff, unless it's about him eating people, and there's only so many cooking shows people can watch.

Now compare Jeff to someone named Sigmund. A Sigmund can't possibly be boring. For instance, did you know that Sigmund Freud's middle name was Schlomo? The dark web will teach you that "Schlomo" is a mix of "shlooha" (Russian for "hooker") and "homo" (Latin for "man"). Sigmund the Man Hooker Freud. How can that story be even remotely boring? You could pitch that to Netflix and you'll get a show with at least two seasons, especially if your character is played by someone who is gay-friendly and easily killable, like Jennifer Coolidge.

Sigmund Freud also came up with such wild theories. According to Freud, little boys are attracted to their mothers, and according to his follower—Carl Jung—little girls are attracted to their fathers. But what Jung and Freud failed to answer is what to call a father attracted to his little girl. Oh, right—Jeffrey Epstein.

Jeremy

I know the name Jeremy is not unlike mine, but I hate it. Unlike me, the letter J is simply unattractive. It looks like a hook, an upside-down 7, and uneven like Jason Biggs's nose.

In fact, everything that starts with the letter J is annoying, such as Japan, Jazz, and even Jehovah's witnesses.

The reason I hate Japan is simple: I hate punctuality. Japan's trains are creepily always on time, so if you're late for work, you can never blame the commute. If I am late for work (which happens often), I sure as hell don't want to hold myself accountable and why I looooooove the subway system in New York City. By the time I get to work, it's time to go home.

Jazz is annoying because there are no lyrics. If you can't put two words together, how stupid are you? Even Ashlee Simpson managed to sing, "La La". Come on Sidney Bechet, try Ta Ta or Ma Ma. Give Daddy something! Blowing into a metal tube is not a skill I stand behind. Plus, a saxophone sounds too raspy for my taste, and if I want raspy, I will visit my aunt who's been smoking for fifty years.

Finally, Jehovah's witnesses. Who are these "witnesses," and what the hell could they have witnessed if Jehovah placed them in the Witness Protection Program way back in 1870? Look, if you've had a secret for one hundred and fifty years, you're no longer a witness. You're just a very old prude who keeps a secret that's no longer relevant. Besides, I already know what "secret" they're trying to hide, which is no secret whatsoever: So what if Hitler had a small, stinky, uncircumcised penis? Everybody in Germany knows that. You could smell his cheesy burrito all the way to Italy. In fact, before Hitler was buried, an Italian entrepreneur swabbed underneath his penis with a Q-tip, and that was the original starter for the nasty Gorgonzola.

John

I hate the name John for various reasons but, primarily, because of Senator John Thune, a Republican whip. He's stupid and self-centered.

He's stupid because his Twitter bio says he "hates shoveling snow," which is stupid. The last time I shoveled snow (with a rolled-up dollar bill) I loved it!

He's self-centered because his Twitter bio says that he's a "father, grandfather, and husband." He's bragging that he's married with children and old enough to have a grandchild. But so what? Like, we can *see* you're old enough to have a grandchild. Tell us something we don't already know. How big is your penis? Does it still work? Have you ever gotten pegged? (Aside from those two times in college.)

The second reason I hate the name John (and especially Jon*) is because of my former friend John. He told me once he was getting a hair transplant in Turkey. If you're losing your hair, roll with it. Bald is sexy! Plus there are starving children in Africa, and here you are spending money left and right to become hairier. If your head gets too cold, instead of wasting $8,000, buy a hat—problem solved.

* Jon or "John with no H" (how they love to be called) is even more annoying. If you don't have something, such as an "H" in your name, there's no reason to be proud of it. You have less—and less is the opposite of more. You've been robbed—so what are you waiting for? Call the police.

Jonathan

Jonathan—like any other long name (or word)—is extremely, tremendously, enormously, impressively, exceptionally narcissistic.

Compare Jonathan, Bernadette, Emmanuelle, Gwendolyn, Rosalinda, Wilhelmina, and Vivienne—to Flo, Jo, Vic, Ty, and Ed. Short and to the point.

I'm a true New Yorker and I love saving space, which is why I don't have time for your florid, lengthy, circuitous, polysyllabic, interminable, serpentine, grandiloquent, agglutinative, stretched-out, dragged-out names.

I met one of such people during a yoga class in London, and his name was Maximilianus Arthur Charles David Windsor IX—and he was a yoga teacher. Long names such as his give you an inflated ego the size of a blimp. Maximilianus was one of those quiet, reserved, wise-looking kinds, with abs and a sexy British accent, and whose life and mental health seemed completely normal compared to mine. Raw, erotic magnetism wafted from his core as if he practices abstinence from sex, while I was on vacation and acted like a whore—the opposite of a vehement, put-together, sagacious yogi with 0 percent body fat. During the class, with my face buried in my mat and my feet in the air, Maximilianus would walk around with a condescending look on his face, correct everybody's pose, and say things like, "Inhale the future, exhale the past" and "I close my eyes in order to see" and "My body is my temple."

I wanted to say, "Yes, Maximilianus, your body is exactly like the temple of Ranakpur in India: beautiful on the outside—and hollow on the inside." Maximilianus, my skinny ass. I thought a shorter name such as Max or Anus suited him better.

Anyhow, back to my friend Jeovanni, who goes by Jonathan. He's trying to make it as an "actor" in New York (which means he's broke and knows how to sing), but he's originally from Brazil (which means he's got a big schlong and looks good in a thong).

I once asked him what his name meant and he said, "Jeovanni means 'father of the sky.'" So his elongated, conceited, four-syllable name essentially means God—the creator of the universe. GOD! Egotistic much?

Oh, and don't give me that whole "My parents named me, so how am I the egotistical one?" speech. You're obsessed with yourself... just like the rest of us.

Kaitlin

My friend Kaitlin has had so much work done, her face has seen more needles than a pincushion. Her face is busier than Walmart on Black Friday. Her lips receive more deposits than Jeff Bezos's checking account. By the way, I'm not judging— I'm just jealous of Kaitlin, because I LOOOOOOOOOVE plastic surgery but don't have the moola for it. If I could afford plastic surgery, trust me, bitch, I'd look tighter than a fitted sheet.

I'm jealous of Justin Jedlica, who's undergone 1,000 plastic surgeries to look like a human Ken doll, because he has all that disposable income. What I don't understand is why copy Ken, a doll with a lockjaw and a full-body Brazilian. If you want to look special, you don't need to cash out your 401-K. All you need is a cut across your face and you'll look like Chucky. Maybe scary, sure, but at least you'll be the only person on the subway who can pull off a "leprechaun in a denim onesie" look.

The most bizarre plastic surgery, in my opinion, is palm line alterations that will allegedly change your fate. Yes, it's true: some idiots have actually had their palm lines changed. Yes, on purpose. A woman I know wanted kids, and after changing the lines on her palms, she got pregnant. No shit, with the amount of money she spent on the surgery, she could no longer afford birth control. And bam—knocked up.

Karl

I hate all Marxist names, including Karl, Leon, Joseph, Fidel, Friedrich, and Vladimir.

Frankly, I *despise* Vladimir Lenin. (Also, I hate that I have to say *frankly* as if otherwise you'll think I'm lying.) I grew up in the Soviet Union—namely Siberia and Kazakhstan—and there were pictures of Lenin all over the place. Every town was either Lenininsk, Leningrad, or Leninogorsk to honor that vain Marxist. How much needier can you get?

The worst Marxist of all time is Mao Zedong. At first, he was humbly known across the world as Mao, but he had to respect his penis by adding Zedong at the end. According to rumors, "Zedong" was no bigger than a large cyst, and one day, the cyst exploded. That's the reason why there are yellow spots on the period-colored red communist flag of China—they're Zedong's pus—to honor him.

Karen

(Yes, the one who needs to speak to the manager.)

Everybody hates the "Karen" haircut for some reason. Why so much hate? Just because Karen is a white, privileged anti-vax soccer mom with an attitude, there's no reason to call her names to her face. Do it behind her back like the rest of us. But if innocent gossip is not enough, do not get nasty or argumentative. Just follow her to Walmart, wait until she gets inside the store, then just friendly slash her tires.

A Karen I know curls her eyelashes so much that her eyes bulge out of their sockets like two golf balls. So now we have a woman named Karen with a Karen haircut plus two golf balls. Doing the math, now we have a woman who will have to play golf, whether she's a member of the golf club or not.

There is no moral to this story except this: Eyelashes protect your eyes. They exist solely for your own good so they can easily catch debris (similar to the way white actors can easily catch Oscar nominations). Your favorite designer—God—created them for a reason. Why are you removing them away from your eyes and asking for trouble? Another golfer will undoubtfully mistake your bulging eyes for a pair of golf balls and will hit them with a putter. And when this happens, you'll go from enjoying a pleasant conversation with a Republican about guns and how much you hate abortions to then sitting in the emergency room with an eye patch discussing whether you should audition for the next installment of *Pirates of the Caribbean*.

Karen, go ahead and talk to the manager of the golf club all you want, but your eye is still blacker than the flag of Al-Qaeda. The only upside of getting hit with a golf club is that you can write a movie about it—*The Catcher in the Eye*. With those bulging peepers of yours, you're perfect to play the part. And—unless you cast someone untalented like Shia LaBeouf or Lea Michelle (which would make the movie tank)—expect the opening weekend to be bigger than Steven Tyler's mouth.

Katie

My friend Katie needs to grow up. No, seriously, she's so short that she's taller than a church.

My point is, why are churches never more than one floor high? With donations pouring in left and right, each church could be as tall as Dwayne "The Rock" Johnson, yet they put up a steeple and call it a day. Adding a steeple to be closer to God is like entering a hotdog-eating contest to lose weight for the summer—it makes no sense!

Plus, tithing is a bad investment for me. So unless you can demonstrate that my money goes to a terrific cause, like making me richer, don't expect me to finance your church endeavors. Listen, if I want to pay money to watch a bunch of people sing songs and stare at an icon, I'll buy a ticket to see Taylor Swift.

Kenya

I love recycling, but I hate it when people recycle names from the globe to a birth certificate.

Kenya is one of those countries I know nothing about, but not due to my ignorance—simply due to my stupidity. I once worked with a girl named Kenya, and I asked her how her name was spelled, and she said, "Exactly like the country in Africa."

I asked, "Which country, Egypt or Uganda?"

She looked at me, rolled her eyes, and walked away.

So I still don't know how her name was spelled.

Kevin

My friend Kevin works for QAnal. No, I didn't misspell QAnon. QAnal stands for "Queer Analytics," an analytical company that examines purchasing trends of queer people.

Their algorithms have been used across all major social media platforms to target ads to the intended demographic.

For example, my Muslim friend Christian sees countless ads for hair trimmers, which makes sense as he's exceptionally bushy. He's the only person I know who's choked on his own hairball.

QAnal's algorithms don't always get it right. My neighbor Scott receives ads for "torn" jeans, a weird trend that makes it look like you've just survived a major car crash. Scott doesn't even own a car.

My pedicurist Greg has been targeted with ads for dumbbells. Yet the only thing he knows how to lift is his face through plastic surgery.

Lastly, my hairdresser Alan gets ads for blow-up dolls, as he's single. By the way, to me blow-up dolls look like elaborate pool floats. What if you mistake one of these sex toys for a drowning person and try to resuscitate it? I won't be caught dead giving mouth-to-mouth to what is basically a balloon.

There's a huge chance it'll burst, and I draw the line at cleaning up rubber bits from a public pool—unless my tetanus shot is up to date.

By the way, I'm disgusted by public pools because they're full of body fluids such as urine, saliva, sweat, nasal discharge, vaginal secretions, and even sperm. Why do you think there are so many teen moms? They go for a swim in itsy-bitsy bikinis and accidentally get impregnated by a free-floating whirlpool of semen. That's why I suggest you wear a wetsuit in any public setting. Sure, you'll look funny, but at least you won't have a screaming toddler in nine months named Kevin.

Kris

The number four is unlucky in Japan, and for that reason, I don't like names with four letters, such as Kris. Not because I'm Japanese but because I'm Russian and superstitious.

For instance, it's considered bad luck when a black cat crosses your path. But when a cat of any color slashes your face, chances are it's your own cat and cats are assholes for no reason. But we still love them . . . because we're stupid.

Here's another one: When your palm itches, it means money is coming, but when your crotch itches, chances are you've slept with Wilt Chamberlain and got an STI. In his autobiography, Wilt claims he's slept with 20,000 women since he was fifteen—that's 1.5 women per day. I don't know about you, but sleeping with 0.06 women per hour sounds impractical. When will I have time to eat?

Lastly*, when you break a mirror, seven years of misfortune will follow, especially if you step on the shards and bleed to death.

* By the way, Lastly, Bigly, and Ugly are another three dwarfs in *Snow White and the Seven Dwarfs* nobody's heard of because they were cut out of the script. Ugly looked like Benedict Cumberbatch, Bigly snacked more than a Teletubby, and Lastly had a lisp, so everyone thought his name was Leslie. When Bigly had eaten through half of the movie budget, the producers slashed the cast, and thank God! For the longest time, I had thought that the idea of seven old perverts hovering over a white woman in a coma was already odd, but *ten* sounds way too tribal. Plus, they're not even doctors as I don't recall seeing any scrubs, and one of them is named Sleepy. Would you trust someone named Sleepy to wake you up from a coma? It's like trusting R. Kelly around underage girls. Also, does it bother no one that the prince kisses a corpse of a fourteen-year-old named Snow? You're a prince, for fuck's sake, so stop being creepy and leave that to

Joachim Kroll. You can't beat twenty years of experience and thirteen victims under his caring wing.

LaToya

I hate LaToya because it rhymes with Goya, and Goya is gross.

Here is my case. On their website, Goya claims they are "authentic Latin cuisine." If by "authentic" you mean "gross, salty, and processed," then authentic it is. What's authentic about vegetable oil, bouillon cubes, and canned beans?

Speaking of their canned beans... I mean who knew that you could monetize on canning farts? I've decided to jump on the bandwagon too, especially since I've been very gassy lately (not unlike Matthew Stonie after feasting on 101 tacos at Chacho's World Taco Eating Championship). Why should I have Gas-X for lunch and waste my precious farts when I could put them in a can and make profit? Lucky for you, my product is authentic, organic, and has zero calories. Just don't forget to rinse the cans before you recycle them.

Case closed.

Laura

(or Lauren, Logan, Lisa, Linda...)

Yes, you're basically the same name since y'all start with the letter L, but like a strange, unorthodox martini, y'all come with a twist.

Have you read Laura Ingraham's book *Of Thee I Zing: America's Cultural Decline from Muffin Tops to Body Shots*?

Nobody has because it's stupid.

Ingraham complains that our forefathers (note: a bunch of rich, white men) would've been appalled had they seen cellphones, skinny jeans, muffin tops, foamy lattes, body shots, and the Kardashians. (Listen, bitch, I grew up in Kazakhstan, which is in Asia just like Armenia, so you don't just come for them, ho—YOU COME FOR ALL OF US.) Ingraham says we've declined culturally in every aspect of our lives, including how we dress, groom, and behave. Ingraham has obviously *never* seen our forefathers.

1) How we dress? Skinny jeans would not be a problem to the forefathers. George Washington's waistcoat was three sizes too small in order to conceal his chubbiness, and because of the laws of physics, whenever you squish one thing, it must reappear elsewhere, so his belly traveled to

his crotch—which is why people thought he packed a massive kielbasa. His breeches were so tight that whenever he jumped on a horse, they ripped at the crotch. The only reason his portraits are from the neck up is because a disaster after a disaster kept happening below the waist.

2) How we groom? Our forefathers' wigs were made out of horse and goat hair and smelled worse than Ozzy Osbourne's breath. Those wigs were powdered with ground lavender to offset the bioaccumulated odor. Don't you think the Johns (Jay, Hancock, and Dickinson) would have rather preferred human lace front wigs similar to ones that look divine on RuPaul?

3) How we behave? First, look at Benjamin Franklin. Not once has he smiled on the $100 bill, yet he still manages to look condescending. With all those $100 bills in circulation, he never even bothered investing in hair plugs.

Also in 1800, it was not uncommon for people to duel each other. That's how Alexander Hamilton died in Weehawken, New Jersey. Do you think that's decent human behavior—to travel to New Jersey?

If you want to live like our forefathers, fine. Start showering once a month and obtain yourself a slave. Then find a mosquito willing to bite you in the ass so you could get sick with yellow fever. And finally, travel everywhere by horse. If a horse is not available, jump on something else that stinks, like the Durian fruit, the White Lives Matter rally, or Boost Mobile service.

Leah

My friend Leah—and hopefully soon "my *former* friend Leah" after she reads my book—is extremely whiny. That makes sense because Leah is a biblical name of Hebrew origin that means "weary." In other words: tired, worn out, exhausted, fatigued, drowsy, spent, jaded, whacked, pooped, enervated . . . I think you get the idea. When you're like all the words on the list above, you have my permission to whine.

On top of that, Leah is also a total Capricorn. In other words: stubborn, impulsive, condescending, skeptical, pessimistic, emotionally unavailable . . . I think you get the idea. I'm not trying to trash Capricorns, but if you're a Capricorn and disagree with what I just said, check the first word on the list—stubborn.

Back to the Bible. In the Old Testament, Leah was married to (note the passive voice) by trickery to a patriarch Jacob. However, Jacob actually loved her younger and more beautiful sister Rachel, whom Jacob later married, leaving Leah "high and dry." "High" from smoking weed to feel better about herself, and "dry" because Jacob took away all her credit cards and Leah could no longer afford a good moisturizer.

So if you're a Leah or a Capricorn, don't be so hard on yourself. It's not your fault you're not as attractive as your sister or that you're skeptical and emotionally unavailable. Blame it on that asshole, Jacob, who betrayed you.

PS, if you fly Spirit Airlines like my friend Leah, then I agree with Jacob and would leave you too.

Leonardo

I hate that lazy asshole, Leonardo da Vinci. He was known to be a slow painter, and many of his works ended up unfinished... except for *The Last Supper*.

Jesus and his twelve followers posed for da Vinci for a whole week while da Vinci took his sweet time, painting a ceiling, of all things. In the mural painting you can notice how everybody is getting tired, cranky, and there is a hazy cloud rising as if their armpits have a pungent smell. Also, if you look closely, you'll see that Jesus has no food on his plate, which is appalling. If someone throws a supper in your honor, the least you can do is ask the waiter to bring you some food—and if not an entrée, at least ask for some salsa and chips.

What most of you don't know is that in the very first rendering of *The Last Supper*, you could see that Jesus has a "third leg," which history books claim was no leg at all. I know you think that a white guy with a big penis sounds like a hoax, which is precisely my point and concrete proof that Jesus was not white.

Anyhow, the "leg" was so massive, the Apostles called him "Jesus and his Willy Wonka." That's exactly why Jesus always wore a dress—because there was no room in a pair of skinny jeans for what he was packing, which according to rumors was "no smaller than a U-Haul truck." (Forget Magnum condoms. Jesus had to use 35-gallon trash bags and lots of duct tape for his sexual encounters.) If you don't believe me, ask the Magic 8-Ball, and you'll get: "All signs point to a yes."

This brings me back to da Vinci. I hate that penis-hating prude, for on the fifth day of drawing, when da Vinci realized "the mysterious third leg" wasn't a leg at all, he painted a STONE SLAB OVER IT, hiding the most interesting, though still questionable, part of Jesus's legacy. So now when you see the final product, the one you can find in the refectory of Santa Marie delle Grazie in Milan, you don't get to see the whole story. What kind of artist fails to show off the most prominent feature? It's like painting Mona Lisa and then accessorizing her with a bike helmet, a face mask, glasses, and finishing her off with the Valencia filter on Instagram; or like painting a bowl of fruit and then . . . just covering it with more fruit.

If you ask the Magic 8-Ball whether Leonardo da Vinci was a complete asshole, you'll get, "Without a doubt."

Lilly

Since Lilly literally means "Lily flower"—so poetic—here's a poem I composed while traveling through South Korea, exploring bathhouses. One night I went out for dinner, and Lilly was my waitress.

> Roses are red.
> My balls are blue.
> My temperature's rising
> 'Cause I've got the flu.

"I'm Lilly," she said,
"I'm your waitress, all right?
I'm thin like a noodle,
And dumb like a kite.

You must be a tourist;
I see a backpack.
You're very attractive
For a hunchback.
I hope you have brought
A big appetite.
A kitten-stuffed dog
Is our special tonight."

I said, "A kitten-stuffed dog
Sounds delicious.
But I'm constipated,
Need something lubricious.
So Lilly, my dear,
Please bring me a beer.
A bagel with schmear,
And expired kefir."

"A kitten-stuffed dog
Will go through you quicker.
It's cooked with anchovies
And basted with liquor."

"Lilly, I trust you.
You seem sincere.
How fresh is the meat?
Was it slaughtered this year?"

"The meat is so fresh
And worth your dough.
The dog was barking
An hour ago."

. . .

I had some leftovers,
Which Lilly packed.
So I understood
Why it's called "doggy bag."

Got back to my room
And wrote in my blog:
"I've just had my first
Korean hotdog."

Liza

I hate Liza because of Liza Minelli. Before you kill me for throwing shade at a gay icon, shut the fuck up and listen.

First, in Siberia, where I am from, if you pronounce her full name—"Liza Minelli"—in Russian it sounds like you're saying, "Liza, we didn't eat." Who would say something stupid like that, a real housewife on Ozempic? Fine, then she could say that, but whom is she speaking to—herself? Frankly, I think she has mental issues. Don't get me wrong, so do I, but I have the decency to stuff my muffin and don't bitch about not eating.

Second, *Minelli* rhymes with the Russian word *pelmeni*, which is what you call a dumpling with meat, and I hate it when people serve me dumplings. Look, if you envelope ground beef into the dough, it takes my stomach twice as long to get the meat out. So half the time, my dumplings come out undigested, and I'm consequently low on protein, and protein supplements are expensive. Besides, if I wanted to eat something inside of something inside of something—I'd gobble a turducken.

I don't have a third point, so now you can close my book and kill me. At least I was able to bitch about something one last time . . .

Louis

I heard this shady story from my friend James who heard it from his friend Amy who heard it from her friend Kate who heard it from her friend Oliver—so it must be true. The name Louis came about when two stupid, lazy, illiterate parents attempted writing Louisiana* on their son's birth certificate, but were oblivious of how to spell the "isiana" part (because they were stupid, lazy, and illiterate like I said) so they left it at Louis. True or not, I'm an avid advocate for shade, so if there's a shady story about two stupid, lazy, illiterate parents, I deem it as real. Anything is possible. Do you remember that incredible tale of Moses spreading apart the Red Sea the way Snoop Dogg spreads Martha Steward's legs? I believe it happened. Maybe it's because I'm a sucker for a miracle. And what's more miraculous than Snoop Dogg spreading Martha Steward's legs?

The name Louis is at the top of my list because it's super confusing. It's pronounced with a hard S at the end: Loo-IS, but when you say LOUISville (Kentucky), all of a sudden it's LOO-ville**.

Similarly, when you pronounce Kansas, you go Kanz-ASS, but for some reason, Arkansas is Arkan-SAW.

Which brings me to Houston Street in NYC that is pronounced HAUS-ton (after William Houston). But for some reason Houston, Texas, is pronounced Humid-As-fuckkkkk.

* I hate that we purchased Louisiana. It cost us 15 million dollars, and ever since then, we've spent another 45 million on legislation. Have you ever googled "weird laws that still exist in Louisiana"? There is a law that makes it illegal to tie horses to trees on a public highway . . . and there's also a law that prohibits you from having sex with a COW. *Wow, how weird,* you're probably thinking. *So tromboning a horse or Rumer Willis is okay?*

Everybody knows (or at least should know) that shagging animals is rape . . . so if you ever wanna toss your hot dog with Bear Grylls, Tiger Woods, or Wolf Blitzer, you're a rapist. Masturbating to animals is frowned upon but often happens by mistake, like when you do it to an alpaca but it's actually a scene with Taylor Lautner. Contrary, having sex with birds is totally acceptable, especially if they're in the Spread Eagle.

** The "loo," by the way, is what the British refer to as the "toilet," so if you happen to drive through LOO-ville, Kentucky, don't forget to urinate right on Main Street.

Lydia

Lydia rhymes with chlamydia, and I don't want to discuss my past.

But I will...

One of the symptoms of chlamydia is a cloudy discharge from the tip of the penis. When I had chlamydia that one time in college, I invited a hookup over and we smoked some weed.

When we got naked, he was like, "Wow, dude, there are clouds coming out of your penis."

"Bro, it's not clouds," I said, "it's just chlamydia."

"What's chlamydia? Will I see a unicorn in the clouds?"

"No, just a urologist at a free clinic."

Marc to Oscar

Marc
Mary
Matthew
Melania
Michael
Mimi
Nathan
Nelsie
Nick
Ocean
Orlando
Osama
Oscar

Marc

Mark with a C is not Marc—it's Carc. I hate names that come with instructions on how they're supposed to be spelled. Which is why I hate it when some stupid asswipe at a party introduces himself as, "I'm Marc with a C" or "I'm John with no H" or "Hi, I'm Zakkkery with three Ks in the middle because my parents are racists and so am I."

Saying things like "I'm Mark with a C," "I'm Jake from State Farm," or "I'm Glen Youngkin, the ugly, stupid governor of Virginia" is extremely egotistical because you've now said more than five words, and I only asked for one—your name. I don't come at you with, "Hi, I'm Jeremy Taylor, a handsome author of the unsuccessful memoir, *Diary of a Mad Gay Man*. I can bench fifty-five pounds at the gym, and I run frequently, the way Joe Exotic runs around the prison with a sore butt."

When someone says, "I'm Mark with a C" while ordering a drink at Starbucks, I can't help but think he's a narcissistic baffoon. Listen, Marc with a C, you frequent that Starbucks every morning, and everyone, including the barista and the janitor, knows you're Mark with a C. Stop whining when someone misspells your name and, please, never post a picture of the cup on Facebook with a caption: "They misspelled Marc *again*!"

What is there to complain about? You can afford to spend five bucks a day on coffee that tastes like something left in a toaster for too long. If you want to spend your money more responsibly, just run it through the garbage disposal.

I've never once complained at Starbucks, even though the last time I was there for a latte, it was a steamingly hot summer day, so I wore a tank top and booty shorts. The barista didn't even ask me for my name. She just wrote "Whore" on the cup.

Also, if you're unhappy with your name, change it. Even celebrities do it. Natalie Portman used to be Natalie Hershlag, Jennifer Aniston's actual last name was Anastassakis, and Kanye West is now Ye (but more like Ney).

And finally, don't misspell common names or insert special characters into them in order to have a "unique" baby name, such as Marc or L!am, Luca$, Will.i.am, ™OTHY, ©arter, J@xon, Ashe®, &rew, 8ob, Coltn●n, or CLLper. Look, if you want to have an "exotic child," adopt one from an exotic place—like Namibia. But if you don't want to go that far (I actually don't know where Namibia is), then shop local, like upstate New York—and trust me, there are lots of weirdos out there. But if you really really really really *really* want a unique baby, a misspelled name simply won't cut it, and you must think broader. For example, a unique baby is a baby that looks really weird and stupid beyond belief. So call Sarah Palin and see where she found Bristol. In a trash can—I'm just guessing.

Mary

Like most names mentioned in this book, Mary is another narcissistic one.

Have you seen *To Catch a Smuggler* on National Geographic? When suspicious-looking people land in the Unites States, the police officers paw through their belongings, trying to find drugs. When that search brings nothing, the officers get frisky and perform a pat-down. When that fails, the officers put on gloves, lube a finger or two, and tell the suspect to bend over. Smugglers smuggle all sorts of drugsy drugs, safely stored inside any body part that comes with an opening, such as their fart box.

"Mary"—and by that I mean whoever was the first Mary on Earth—has similarly stuffed herself in every word in the dictionary just so she can hear herself whenever someone opens their flap: rosemary, calamary, summary, primary, Maryland, spermary*... and many more.

When her plan became too obvious, Mary went further and created homophones to stay inconspicuous: Marry, merely, marinade, marriage, and I find that quite narcissistic.

My point is Mary is a smuggler and she's just been caught! So give me a moment to bitch about every Mary my small mind can think of.

First, let's talk about Bloody Mary, a delicious cocktail with vodka, tomato juice, and a ton of healthy vegetables such as pickles, celery, and horseradish. Surely it was invented by a mother so her kids could 1) eat more vegetables and 2) quickly pass out. There's nothing wrong with that, except I'd also throw in some Benadryl, so not only the kids would 3) pass out quicker but also 4) sleep longer. But one question, why call it a Bloody Mary? Next time just order a Menstruating Mary at the bar. Instead of celery, it comes with a stick of tampon.

Next, Mary Magdalene or Mary MAGAdalene as she may as well be called because she was a Trump supporter and here's why: According to Encyclopedia Britannica, Mary watched Jesus's crucifixion... which is such a MAGA move. What kind of pervert *was* she? If you're into watching people get crucified, there's no limit to your cruelty. What's next for Mary? Will she start kicking homeless kittens, watching Fox News, and womanspreading on the subway? Also, have you ever seen Mary Magdalene? If not, google her pictures. On each one of them she's kneeling before Jesus Christ. So what if she knows how to give head? Big deal. But that's not a skill she should proudly put on her résumé. Other than watching a guy getting stamped to a cross, can she sew, bedazzle, or at least do a cartwheel?

How about Mary, Queen of Scots? The dodo apparently washed her face with white wine . . . yet never shared it with anyone, not even friends. What a selfish, egotistical, wine-wasting daughter of a bitch.

Last, I want to talk about my college friend Mary whom I lovingly refer to as "the cheap ass." Once, we went out to dinner and I got the least expensive appetizer to save money, but she ordered the porterhouse and the lobster, plus three twenty-dollar martinis. When the check arrived she asked, "Should we split it?"

Split it? Is she crazy? I told her I'm not a ballerina or a drag queen and I don't do splits, and if she's still looking for one, I could split her neck. Mary explained she was saving for "a rainy day." *And what*, I wanted to ask, *pay only when it's sunny?* Fine. So now I only hang out with Mary during the summer.

So last summer, she and I** had a picnic in Central Park, but, of course, Mary was being Mary—complicated and annoying and allergic to EVERYTHING. Dog hair, cat hair, seafood, dairy, gluten, sesame ... The only thing she's not allergic to is air—which is unfortunate. I wanted Mary to pay me back for the "rainy day" dinner, so that day I had made an amazing potato salad for the picnic (and I said it was allergen-free, but it wasn't), so Mary swelled up, swallowed a chunky piece of carrot, and chocked. I did the Heimlich, patted her on the back, and said "Bless you."

Her red, swollen face stared at my pale, beautiful one, and she said, "*Bless* me? But I didn't *sneeze*!"

She's just never satisfied, is she?

I said, "My apologies, Mary. I'm so ignorant. I meant to say 'Kiss my ass, I hope you die.'" She didn't, but that's OK. There'll always be another summer.

The only reason Mary and I are still friends is because she's gorgeous and I can't stand ugly people. Every time I see her I dial God and say, "Gosh, God, she's so beautiful—heaven must be missing an angel." But then God dials me right back and says, "Nope, we're just missing a whore."

* *Spermary* is a word that means "an organ in which male gametes are developed," so a flowery way to describe balls. I hate flowery ways. If you need to say "balls," say "balls." If you need to say, "dress appropriately," don't say "wear smart casual." (Clothes, like anyone trying to oppose Putin, can't

be smart.) Last, if you need to say "a fucking nightmare," just say "Mary."

** Yes, it's "she and I" and not "she and me"—look up the difference, you uncultured fools. And while you're at it, do not use apostrophes for plural nouns. "Bitch" is singular. "Bitches" is plural. If you ever again write "bitch's" when referring to my seven personalities, I will block you on Facebook—especially if you're homely.

Matthew

Matthew is a Biblical Hebrew name that means "Gift from God." Really? A gift from God—*a gift*? A screaming white baby named Matthew that keeps me up at night is not a gift—it's a nightmare. A gift is a two-carat diamond ring from Tiffany's, a nonstick pan from Williams Sonoma, or a barber who doesn't talk.

Dear God, if you're listening to me, please send me a real gift. You're Almighty and stuff, and I know you have the power to do something more extraordinary than sending all these Matthews my way. And since I've lived in New York for way over ten years, I've met my fair share of Matthews.

How? Let's just say that when you have a nice, bouncy ass like mine, people approach you often, and because I have no standards, I talk to everyone.

So, God, if you could grant me the following three wishes, in return feel free to assassinate any three Matthews from my Facebook—just make it quick and painless—and don't leave a trail.

Here's what I need, God.

One: Make overfishing more popular. Do you know how much mercury is in a can of tuna? Neither do I, but I assume lots. But did you know that mercury is used in the production of gold? And my thinkage is that the more fish we eat, the less gold there is to go around, which will raise its street value. God, I have thirty gold teeth to pawn after we cremated Grandma—and the rent is due . . .

Two: God, please end hunger. Not world hunger, no. Pease end hunger in my stomach so I could finally lose some weight. I am tired of all that jelly in my belly. I need some slim in my limb.

Three: God, please stop child labor. I hate that children who are forced to work are not paying taxes, which means there's less money to go around for local improvements. Potholes in New Jersey are out of fucking control!

Melania

Do you know how Melania Trump ended up in the United States? Back in Slovenia, she was watching *Shrek* in 3D. As you know, 3D glasses are blue and red, similar to the United States, and being colorblind to human decency and kindness, Melania picked the red side—the Republican one.

On the bright side, Melania is a true patriot because she supports immigrants by depleting the U.S. budget . . . If you're confused, bear with me.

Let's start with the White House State Dinner for Emmanuel Macron, during which Melania (together with Tiffany and Donald) put away a massive amount of food, from farm-raised lamb to lobster to imported fromage to Skinny Girl margaritas. Melania was storing up for winter not unlike a bear before hibernation—and that alone cost the country an arm and a leg. In addition, Melania wasted millions on planting some roses at the Rose Garden, billions to redecorate the White House for Christmas, then she shelled out a fortune on extra security every time she was shopping at Walmart or chartered Air Force One. All that money added up to a thirty-trillion-dollar debt. In fact, when it comes to spending taxpayer money, Melania is busier than Times

Square on New Year's Eve; busier than Genene Jones on a killing spree; even busier than me making up dad jokes:

> Which ale is the healthiest ale? Kale.
>
> Where deals are made? Dealaware.
>
> What is the strongest wine? Twine.

Back to my point—how Melania helped immigrants. With all the money she was squandering, there wasn't much dough left for the Mexican wall, and BAM, immigrants could finally cross the border. And being an immigrant myself, I support that fully.

PS: For those of you who don't know, so most of you, Genene Jones—better known as "angel of death"—poisoned sixty children—SIXTY—and is now serving time in prison. The one thing that stands out, aside from all the dead children, of course, is her nickname, which starts poetically—*angel* . . . and then BAM—*of death*. I for one hate oxymorons such as this and "angel of death" sounds worse to me than "original copy" or "small crowd." Think about it, *Small . . . crowd*. Are you *that* stupid that you can't come up with a decent synonym? Small *gathering*, perhaps? Unless you mean it literally as in "a crowd of small people" (like those children poisoned by Genene Jones), then it's OK to use it—but otherwise shut your trap! The only oxymoron I love using is "pretty ugly," because then I know we're talking about Macaulay Culkin. By the way, I apologize for venting and being rude—I'm just always angry. If you ever want to catch me in a good mood, then watch me sleep.

Michael

Let's talk about that litterbug, Michael Jackson. He tried throwing a baby—a whole baby—out of his balcony, and if he could do that, imagine how much other trash he threw out?

The Earth is literally dying because people like Michael Jackson don't know how to recycle. For example, to save the planet, I use reusable straws and avoid plastic bags. The least you could do is use an appropriate bin for your fucking baby.

Look, if you don't want your baby, fine, but don't throw it out. At least put it up for adoption, donate it to Goodwill, or buy a bucket and send it down the Hudson River. Who knows, perhaps it'll become another Mowgli. And if there's a movie deal, you're rich!

Mimi

I hate all names that keep multiplying like bacteria from the same building block, such as Mimi, Cece, Fifi, Jojo, Kiki, Juju, Koko, Nini, Vivi, Zizi, Zuzu, and Pippi.

It's like playing the same note over and over, and it hurts my ears. Besides, I hate narcissistic names, and Mimi sounds like, "Me, me!" We get it, Mimi, and we can see you. At 150 pounds you're not translucent. So stop crying for attention.

By the way, Mimi comes from French and means "sea of bitterness," a whole sea of it. Imagine a sea of coffee without milk or sugar, just a bitter black sea that gives you diarrhea and bad breath. That's Mimi—bitter and narcissistic.

Nathan

Nathan was the name of my ex-boyfriend.

Here's how we broke up—on our third date. We went to get massages together in a Korean neighborhood, which is in the northern part of town, so in a sense you could say we were in North Korea. I always go to the same place because I'm a loyal bitch.

My massage therapist is, unsurprisingly, Korean, especially with a name such as Dong-Hyun. He's maybe forty and five feet tall, but stronger than he looks. His knot-removal technique—by poking me with his elbows—leaves me screaming in pain, which is why Dong-Hyun told me I sound louder than a Russian woman getting a Brazilian. On the contrary, his toe-rubbing technique is way too ticklish, and I wiggle all over the massage table, cackling more than Courtney Love on elephant tranquilizers. Between crying from pain and laughing from pleasure, I always leave the session sore, loopy, and disoriented.

That day, Nathan was getting a massage in the next room, while I was getting massaged/punished/tickled by Dong-Hyun. At the end of the session, I asked if Nathan would cover the massage and I would cover our dinner later that night. Nathan paid.

As soon as we made it outside, Nathan asked me, "Are you cheating?"

I said, "On my diet? Of course not!"

He said, "I mean, did you sleep with Ding Dong?"

I said, "Well, first of all his name is Dong-Hyun, and second of all, it's only one in the afternoon. Why would I be sleeping? It's not like we went to the brewery again and I passed out in the bathroom."

Nathan said, "I don't want to dance around the issue—"

I interrupted, "Why not? Is that because you don't know how to dance? You know you could take some classes or watch a few seasons of *Dancing with the Stars*."

He breathed out REAL deep and said, "Did you have sex with Dong-Hyun?"

"Sex?" I asked. "He's as attractive as a guy in a onesie."

Nathan said, "But I heard the same noises you make in the bedroom."

"Was I snoring?"

He said, "You need help, Jeremy."

I said, "I know. That's why I came here. My knots are out of control."

He said, "Let me put it another way: Did you get a happy ending?"

I said, "Not *Pretty Woman* happy, but more like *Marley & Me* happy. The ending was: I cried at the end."

He said, "I heard really loud slurping."

I said, "Oh, it was probably Dong-Hyun eating ramen. He told me his asshole boss doesn't give them time for lunch, so Dong-Hyun eats whenever he walks on my back. I don't mind. Hey, I also love multitasking—what a genius way to save time."

He said, "We're breaking up, Jeremy."

I hadn't realized we were speaking on the phone. So I said, "Why are we breaking up? You think the reception is bad in this part of town? Should we try texting?"

He said, "You're stupid," then got in his car and drove off....

Long story short, since Nathan paid for the massage I saved fifty bucks! I invested it, and now it's doubled. So who's stupid now, huh?

Nelsie

Yes, it's a name. I couldn't believe it either so I had to look it up. As I'm typing this on my computer, it keeps underlining the name in red as if it's misspelled. And this is a lesson for all y'all—before naming your child Kingmessiah, Xxavyer, KKK, or worse, Nelsie, type it in a Word document. If it's underlined—change it. Easy peasy lemon squeezy.

So here's something none of you know, as y'all stupid: To see which names are popular for any given year, go to the Social Security Administration's website and search through their database. That's where I learned that Nelsie is a rare name—with less than a hundred and twenty recorded in the last century by the Social Security Administration. But if you search Liam, Olivia, Bobby, Antonio, Camilla, Kelly, and literally every name in this book, those names are apparently as common as hemorrhoids and vegans who are annoying.

I did some research for you—because I'm awesome—and here's what I found:

The most popular names in 1918 were Paella and Gazpacho, celebrating the Spanish flu.

Under Eisenhower, in 1953, when Alaska and Hawaii became states, parents who traveled to Alaska would often name their children White Trash, and those traveling to Hawaii named their kids Leia, Beautiful Beaches, and What a Long Flight!

And finally, in 1993 when there was a 51-day gun standoff in Waco, Texas, between a religious cult and the FBI, the most common names were Holy Shit and I had No Idea It Was so Easy to Buy a Gun.

My editor, Nelsie—whom I adorably refer to as "Ugh, she again" and whose laugh is more annoying than the sound of Santa trying to fit his ass through the chimney—has butchered this book. She deleted everything I wrote, saying, "You can't say this," "You can't say that," "This is sexist," "This section is straightaphobic," "This paragraph is rude and racist," "You have to write a new book called *One Hundred and Eleven People I Love*."

First of all, I'm not a fucking hippy. "Love" is a strong word which I abhor because people overuse it, diminishing its meaning. When it comes to using that word myself, here are the things I LOVE: bacon, hamburgers, fries, mimosas, summer, running, having sex with random people without getting STDs, *I Love Lucy*, celebrity breakups, Oprah, gossip, another funeral with a buffet . . . But *people*? *Love?* Don't be ridiculous. The only person I love (aside from my Amazon delivery guy as I love receiving packages) is Ivan, my imaginary friend, because he is deaf and can't argue with me.

Second, is that what you wanted to hear, Nelsie, that you're right? You don't need to be a genius to understand that my book is indeed rude and sexist and yada, yada, yada. When I write, I like being honest with people—that I hate them. It's only when I see you (and other people) in person, I smile and say, "Good to see you." But, please, think about it? What's *good* about seeing you, people? Have you met . . . *you*?

Nick

Nick was the name of a guy I dated who is from Chunky, Mississippi,* and we broke up because Nick was in the military and wasn't allowed to date a Russian guy because, as he put it, "You could be a spy." That's so pessimistic. *Anyone* could be a spy/serial killer/sadist/vegan/or worse—a Gemini. You gotta stay positive! For instance, if you see a toothless white man in a wife beater in Denver, Colorado, instead of wondering if he's homeless, ask yourself why wife beaters look so hot on guys with tattoos. That analogy was very dumb, but this is a dumb book... My point is, thinking someone is a spy based on his nationality is like cooking spaghetti in a toaster—it makes NO sense.

Back to Chunky, Mississippi... I believe Chunky is a rude and fat-shaming name. Nick explained that Chunky was originally named after Adele. But now that Adele has lost weight, Chunky's mayor has proposed three new possible titles for the municipality: Seethrough, Cheekbones, and Madison Cawthorn.

The last one has nothing to do with Adele. You see, Chunky has natural deposits of sulfur, so when it came to honoring the town's stench, North Carolina representative, Madison Cawthorn, immediately came to mind.

* I still don't understand why we have to spell "Mississippi" upon getting pulled over. Look, there are harder words to spell such as chiaroscurist, hors d'oeuvre, gonorrhea... But Mississippi? Unless you're a toddler, spelling a word constructed out of four letters should be fairly easy. Other field sobriety tests are just as stupid. You either walk in a straight line or stand on one leg. What if you ONLY have one leg or can't walk in a straight line because you're a "twisty" little bitch? So as you can see, the system is flawed.

Me, I don't need any tests. Here's how I know when a woman is drunk: You just know.

Here's how I know when a man is drunk—his penis stops working (not unlike Santa on December 26th). So if you're a cop who wants to do a good job—start touching!

Ocean

Naming a baby Ocean is like naming it Garbage. There's so much plastic, aluminum, and medical waste in our oceans, they've become more disgusting than white trash eating Spam fries and green bean casseroles in Tuscaloosa, Alabama.

The Atlantic is filthy, and the last time I was on Brighton Beach, people urinated straight into the ocean, because . . . why not? Also, that's where the RMS *Titanic* had an affair with a married iceberg, whose husband found out and cut the bitch, sinking the damn thing.

Did you know that RMS stands for Royal Mail Ship? What a shame that all that mail got lost. Imagine how many people in America never got the chance to read the news from Europe. The answer is: a lot.

Plus, a few or so people died that day too, but I think it was by choice. There were life vests and lifeboats, after all! Don't get me wrong, the fish had a blast at the buffet—Spanish cuisine? You got it. Royal ladyfingers? Coming right up. French tips? Knock yourself out!—but why train the fish by giving them free food? Since then, the fish have had high expectations, and they've stopped hunting altogether, which is why depression in the fish community is at an all-time high.

One time my friend Kate fell overboard, right next to a Cow shark. When the shark realized Kate was a shrink, it sat down on a chair and said, "Doctor Kate, I'm very depressed! I'm so fat I look like a cow!" Kate diagnosed the shark with seasonal affective disorder and charged it $175.

Orlando

Similar to state names like Virginia, Dakota, and Carolina, I hate town names like Orlando, Phoenix, and Vienna.

For example, why Phoenix? If you throw your baby in a fire and it comes out flying, sure, name it Phoenix, but otherwise, forget it.

Vienna? After Vienna sausages? Don't punish your baby just because you're a glutton and wanted a cocktail wiener.

Orlando is a city in Florida whose official nickname is "The City Beautiful." What's beautiful about it? Sure, there are a hundred lakes all around, but that also means a hundred places where gators can be lurking. There's nothing fun about a cold-blooded predator with prickly fangs. If I wanted to get pierced by something sharp, I'd get a nose ring right here in New Jersey.

By the way, Orlando's basketball team is the Orlando Magic. I don't know about you, but I see nothing magical about basketball, as I have no interest in watching a bunch of men abusing a spherical object. In fact, the world leaders are doing the exact same thing to our planet. Global issues are only growing, like the number of facelifts on Nicole Kidman. Just read the news: pollution, hunger, and the gender wage gap. Men DON'T deserve more money simply because there are extendable gadgets in their pants that think on their own. Similar to artificial intelligence, if penises could detach, they would take over the world. Frankly, I see an enormous problem with schlongs on the loose. Since they're smaller than rats, their population will get out of control, and with no paws or saliva to scrub themselves, I can only imagine how much they'll stink. Worse than Iggy Pop's armpits.

Wouldn't it be better if women governed the land, like the fabulous Marie Antoinette? Addicted to gambling and fashion, she was a spendthrift and promiscuous beyond belief, eerily similar to the Tasmanian devil during the mating season—just less screaming and biting.

But Ivan the Terrible? As his name implies, he was terrible—because he executed disloyal traitors by boiling and roasting them alive. What terrible about that was actually his cooking. For example, you never boil a steak before you grill it as it loses its flavor. Plus, Ivan the Terrible never used any seasoning, and according to Julia Child just a tad of herbes de Provence with a splash of Cabernet is all you need to make a mean *boeuf bourguignon*. His cooking was so terrible even the least fussiest eaters, such as pigeons, would not touch it. One time a vulture tried it, discharged it through his anus, and only then pigeons would eat it, saying it was finally well-seasoned.

The fact that Ivan the Terrible roasted people alive is actually a true story, and I believe so because fat kills. He died from a stroke, which is proof he failed to follow the FDA dietary guidelines—as after all, human steaks are a galore of fat, and fat from red meat blocks your arteries—and BAM—a stroke.

In Russian, his last name is Grozny, which comes from the word "groza," which literally means "lightning." Ivan the Lightning doesn't have the same gravitas as Ivan the Terrible, does it? But I think the name Ivan the Terrible Cook or Ivan the Paula Deen suited him better.

Osama
(bin Laden. Who the fuck else?)

Oof, this will be a hard one, but bear with me . . .

Let's talk about Osama bin Laden's generous nature. The TSA was founded two months after 9/11. Bin Laden's humble dream was to introduce yoga to the world, which is why we now do the downward dog at the airport while removing our shoes.

I'm not a believer in free things, like free yoga lessons. Whenever something is too good to be true, follow the money. How does bin Laden benefit from us stretching before our flights? Simple: he knew how many of us dreaded flying, and he simply wanted us to relax before our flights without drugs or alcohol—because alcohol is forbidden in Islam. Clearly, Osama's ultimate goal was to put the alcohol industry out of business . . . which is noble and sweet. But not for a Russian. So I'm happy the scuzzbag was shot.

PS: Speaking of yoga: I don't know about you, but stretching in a room full of sweaty people on a dirty mat is far beyond unsanitary. If you simply like to hang out in an unhygienic environment full of stinkage, visit the men's locker room at Planet Fitness.

Oscar

Every celebrity in Hollywood hates the name Oscar because most of them never receive one.

I hate the week leading up to the Oscars because celebrities stop eating food to look their best on camera, and local restaurants suffer. The only person who still eats is Armie Hammer because he doesn't have a career. But what a hot piece of ass, huh?

By the way, keep in mind, that if you name your baby after transportation (such as Os-CAR), that alone will make your baby a celebrity. Here's proof: Meghan Trainor, Rick Shaw, Trammy Lee Jones, Katy Ferry, Busta Rhymes, and Queen Planetifah.

Patrick to Ryan

Patrick
Pearl
Phillip
Pierce
Pinocchio
Quigley
Quin
Ramy
Reign
Rhett
Rosa
Rudy
Ryan

Patrick

My plumber Patrick is overweight and insecure about it. What's there to be insecure about? Simply put, your body has created some extra cells, so what? Think of yourself as a fancy spreadsheet.

Short story long, don't take fat-shaming personally. Weight is unstable and unpredictable, like Roseanne Barr on Ambien. And if you're ever called fat, you should first understand where the bullies come from. People become tyrants for one main reason—small dog syndrome—and they take it out on you because they are jealous. For instance, my neighbor's tiny Chihuahua never stops barking whenever she sees me. That's because she's jealous that *I'm* the biggest bitch in the building.

Pearl

Pearl is a white, spherical, shiny object, and if your baby looks like that, I see no reason why not to call her Pearl.

My friend Daisy, for example, told me that when she was born, she had a yellow face (thanks to jaundice) and white hair. My other friend said his parents had no idea whether he was a boy or a girl, so they called him Chance. And my friend Ruby simply was born with a red sheen in her cheeks.

All the above names are fine, just unoriginal. So if your baby comes out white and yellow, perhaps with an occasional stripe, forget Daisy. Instead, call her Wallpaper from the 50s.

If your baby could be either a boy or a girl, don't take a chance. Call it We'll Decide in a Few Years.

And if your baby is white with red undertones, don't be too obvious with Strawberry, Cabernet, or Fire Truck. Try an unusual name—Used Tampon.

Phillip

I hate it when parents chose baby names containing body parts, such as Armaan, Legend, Earnest, Nail, Phillip, and Neckah. Are you insinuating that your child has arms, legs, ears, nails, lips, and a neck, while other kids in your child's class resemble fish? Everybody on Earth has the above-mentioned body parts, with three exceptions.

One, Kristen Dunst barely has any lips left. Maybe Jesse Plemons has a penis sharper than a grater, and Kristen's lips keep getting smaller and smaller from giving blowjobs.

Two, Evander Holyfield lost his ears after Mike Tyson feasted on them.

And three, the Olsen Twins have no necks* because they were "Whack-A-Moled" too many times on Coney Island.**

Speaking of necks and islands, in northwestern Thailand, women of the Padaung tribe stretch out their necks using heavy brass rings, which is why their necks are the longest in the world. I think it's a waste of time, and here's why: It already takes forever and a half for my food to travel through my esophagus. Stretch the neck any longer, and I'll starve to death by the time borscht reaches my stomach. I don't know about you, but I'm a Millennial, so I don't have three hours for a fucking lunch. And if I ever must stretch something on my body, it'll be skin on my face through an extensive facelift.

Pierce

Pierce is an overrated name because I've heard it a billion times. Be original and name your child Puncture, Perforation, or Penetration instead.

Peirce carries a violent connotation that Penetration doesn't. When King Charles attempted canceling Christmas on January 30, 1649, he got executed by getting pierced to death. My point is, if King Charles had gotten penetrated instead, he would've stayed alive—sore in the butt, but alive.

By the way, Pierce means "rock," derived from the Greek word *pétros*. That explains why my former roommate Pierce—who resembled a rocky Eichelman Beach in Wisconsin—was dirty, disgusting, and lots of naked people visited him.

Pinocchio

(Yeah, yeah, yeah, I know that nobody would name their child Pinocchio—unless they have sex with Woody Allen and their baby comes out wooden. While we're on the subject, what kind of name is Woody?)

So if your baby does—magically, mysteriously, miraculously—come out wooden, before naming it Pinocchio make sure the baby is not made out of bamboo. Bamboo grows to its full height in only three years. I just can't imagine your three-year-old applying for college and moving out.

However, if the baby is pine or a Saguaro cactus, you're in luck. It takes seventy years for a cactus to bloom, and there's hardly any maintenance. Sure, your baby will be painful to hug, but think of it as "needling," for which my chiropractor charges a fortune and a quarter.

And hey, if you're ever strapped in the desert, your baby is 90 percent water. You're no longer thirsty!

Quigley

There are four words women hate the most: curd, moist, flap, and discharge. All common dictionary words, so no need to get upset. But for some reason, women like words that rhyme, such as squiggly, wriggly, and Quigley (which is a perfect name for an ugly baby or a Boston Terrier).

So let's make a deal. Men, promise to never use the four words that make women cringe; and women, promise to never say the four words that men abhor: "We need to talk."

Quin

Quin is not a name but a prefix to Quinton, Quintrell, Quintus, and obviously, QuinANON. My point is, avoid naming your child after a prefix. The prefix "Anal" works similarly in Analee, which is not a name but a sexual position.

I have a friend whose name is Quin. He's a professor at a Plumbing School and he uses long, annoying words and expressions such as "meretricious," "celerity," and "the opening at the end of alimentary canal"—when simply "pretentious," "fastness," or "asshole" would do.

Quin once said he suffers from Stockholder syndrome.

I asked, "You mean Stock*holm* syndrome?"

He said, "No, Stock*holder* syndrome. I'm scared of investing because I don't want to be a stockHOLDER." Look, I'm not surprised. What did you expect would happen to somebody named after a prefix like Quin?

Ramy

According to the Internet, the meaning of Ramy is all over the place: "loving," "archer," and "father of multitudes."

How do you go from a "loving" sweetheart—to someone who shoots arrows—to a rapist impregnating slutty mademoiselles who later becomes a father of multitudes?

When it comes to names, pick a meaning and for fuck's sake stick to it. For example, Olive means "olive," and Rose means "rose," and both are VERY EASY—which is why, I guess, Ramy impregnated them.

My friend Ramy is a paparazzo—meaning he's a pervert who knows how to stalk, yet rich enough to have a nice camera. One time he showed me a picture of what looked like a white trash bag but ended up being a picture of Tiffany Trump. And another time he showed me a picture of what looked like Alabama Senator Katie Britt, but ended up being a picture of a white trash bag.

I guess it's true what they say, "An apple a day won't change the fact that you're garbage." If you're wondering who said that, close the book and see the author's name on the cover.

Reign

Reign sounds like you're saying "rain," but what if I forgot my umbrella?

Besides, be sure your child's name rhymes with *nothing*, or otherwise, bullies will make fun of it: "Reign has no brain, and she's a vain shitstain who sniffs cocaine. Frankly, she's insane!"

Do you see what I mean? But try to find a word that rhymes with Opus or Discombobulate. Sure, they're not names—yet. But there's always room for inventions. Before

Gwyneth Paltrow and Jason Lee, Apple and Pilot Inspektor hadn't existed. And after the Kardashians we are left with Psalm, Saint, Dream, True, Chicago, North West, and—yes—Reign.

My former coworker Reign was a pale redhead like a mix between Annie and the Pillsbury Doughboy, and like a dolphin, she always smiled and made weird, squeaky noises. Reign told me she was born prematurely and came out two weeks early, which is ironic as now she's always late (not dissimilar to the M25 bus that goes to LaGuardia). She also refuses to wear a bra for her giant breasts and her nipples stick out like two light switches—and like math or geology—are very hard. She and I worked at a Halloween store, and one time when Reign saw a guy buying a Spiderman costume she said, "Spiderman's *so* hot. I would *so* ride his bony express."

I thought that was so dumb of her. Spiderman climbs walls, and like a true spider that's where he'd have sex—on a ceiling or a side of a building. I think those are dangerous places for an intercourse unless you have spidery fingers, which Reign didn't. Spiderman would bring Reign on top of the Chrysler Building for some privacy and before he could put on a condom, Reign would fall down like a giant asteroid and splatter all over the sidewalk, causing a minor earthquake. My advice? No climbing while stuffin' the muffin—unless you want your last word to be "AHHHHHHH!"

Rhett

The letter H in Rhett, Rheged, and Rhadamanthus is silent. Adding silent letters to make a name memorable is like gaining extra pounds to lose weight—stupid.

What bothers me is that Rhett is considered normal, but other names with silent letters are not: Phlegm, Mnemonic, and Pterodactyl. We should be more inclusive and bring those names into circulation too. Sure, most people won't understand them, but most people also don't understand how plumbing works—yet we shit anyhow.

I once dated a Rhett, and he was the most annoying Rhett on Earth (aside from Rhett Butler*) because Rhett used metaphors excessively. If you've read this book thus far, you've learned how much I hate figurative language. He was a cab driver and referred to his car as "his office." Sure, he spends HOURS in his car, but a space is not technically considered an office unless you can steal something from it. (What can you possibly steal from your own car?) If you're a cab driver, please don't say after lunch, "It's time to go back to the office," trying to be funny. Look, my brother is a plumber, but he never deducted a plunger from his taxes because it was an "office supply."

Rhett would mutter other absurd sentences like, "I have no words," and then resume gabbing, or he'd preface with, "I'm gonna be honest"... like his mama never taught him that he should always be honest. Unless you talk about someone's baby when you MUST MUST MUST be fake and comment on how cute their bald, crying, toothless baby—who looks like a piglet in a blanket—is.

The dealbreaker (and a breakup) was when Rhett metaphorically described his sister as "not the sharpest knife in the drawer." I appreciated the fact he spoke shit about his sister behind her back (like I do about my friends and relatives), but never—under any circumstances—use culinary metaphors on a trained chef. For days I kept thinking about how dangerous it is to use a dull knife.

This is the 21st century, and people don't have time for pompous language, and unless you're a writer (or a GOOD writer like me), there's no need for your Shakespearian amateurisms. So if your sister is stupid, then say so. Don't say she fell out of the family's tree, her chimney's clogged, or that her antenna doesn't pick up all the channels. Because all I'll think about is a woman falling from a tree, a clogged chimney, and a TV without HBO.

* Rhett Butler is on my shitlist because he was dumb enough to marry Scarlet O'Hara, arguably the most obnoxious woman in literature. Akin to most wealthy people, Scarlet was frugal, and to avoid spending money at a spa,

she would occasionally ask the maid to vacuum her for some slap-me-mama-good suction treatment, followed by a gentle cleanse with their newly acquired Swiffer. And when O'Hara's yet another husband would articulate that her hairy chupacabra was ready for an upkeep, she'd traipse around the plantation and the gardener would prune her. With at least three husbands that we know of, her insatiable beaver had stored so much wood, the wood eventually ignited, and boom, Atlanta's burning.

At the end of *Gone with the Clunge*, I mean *Gone with the Wind*, Scarlet yammered, "Tomorrow is another day."

CLEARLY tomorrow is another day, you stupid hag. Even Dog the Bounty Hunter would never utter a thing like, "Tomorrow I'm still ugly"—because everybody knows that. Such obviosity is beyond ridiculous. I don't approach a random stranger in the middle of Times Square and beg for money; I just steal their wallet. And whenever I want to impress somebody and take their breath away, I don't dress nicely; I just press my foot against their throat. And when I pull my hands up, I don't tell a police officer, "Don't shoot, don't shoot! Can't you see I'm white?"

Anyhow, I've lost my point . . . but I've also lost dignity, credibility, and reputation. And yes, I tried contacting Lost & Found at Penn Station, and you know what they said? They said, "If you're looking for dignity, credibility, and reputation, you must be Marjorie Taylor Greene."

Rosa

My friend Rosa is an environmentalist and doesn't believe in using A/C. She says Freon—an odorless gas and the key ingredient in A/C refrigerants—depletes the ozone layer. *So what?* That's why the layers exist in the first place! But unlike Mama June, Mama Earth isn't stupid and had created several coatings so we could use them now, not a thousand years later. Rosa thinks she's noble like Rosa Parks, but she's more like a parked car on top of roses—she makes no sense.

Rosa argues that if those layers keep disappearing, celestial objects will start falling from the sky. *So what?* Worrying about hypotheticals is like worrying whether your descendants will be trashy just because you once visited El Paso or farted in a crowded elevator.

So what if glaciers are melting, CO_2 levels are rising, and the ozone layer is fading? By the time something bad happens, you and everyone you know will be dead. So enjoy your A/C and let future generations worry about consequences.

Like my mama used to say, "The hangover is tomorrow, but the party is tonight!"

Rudy

I actually love the name Rudy... but only for a female stripper.

I'm tired of overused stripper names that end with "-dy" such as Kandy, Brandy, or Cassidy. Which is why I'd like to put in rotation Rudy, Winifred, and Agnes as possible stripper names. Sure, Rudy would probably be seventy years young (yes, old people tend to say that) but, in my opinion, age is just a number. The real reason older people don't seek employment in exotic dancing is not because they think they're too old. It's because insurance doesn't cover "falling from a stripper pole," so they're being cautious. After all, hip replacements are costly. My stripper friend Coco, for example, forgot to chalk her hands before doing a spin and flew through the room and got a concussion. Now instead of Coco, she's just poco loco + one broken arm.

My next-door neighbor Rudy is a singer who believes one day he'll be on *The Voice*. I think he belongs on *Hoarders*. He doesn't throw anything out and his apartment, like dreads on Justin Bieber, is a complete disaster.

When I first met him, he told me to ask him anything and that he was, as he put it, "an open book." He indeed was like a book, like several books, actually: *All My Friends Are Dead*,

The Muffin Muncher, *The Hobbit*. I'll also throw in *Planet of the Apes* and if you saw his face you'd agree. Look, I'm not trying to be mean. As a writer, I simply describe people to my best ability and, fortunately, my best ability is knowing how to be mean. So let's continue.

Rudy's face resembles the surface of the moon: shiny, uneven, and "it's just there," and nobody seems to care much about it. In fact, he's so ugly, his only dates are either in his calendar or come wrapped in prosciutto. The only time he plays with pussy is when he visits a cat shelter. He's so stupid, he thinks "Turkish delight" is that hot girl selling kabobs on the corner of Greene and Monroe. I once introduced him to my friend Dakota, and Rudy asked, "North or South?"

What I'm trying to say is this: Whenever I think of being friends with my neighbor Rudy, I think of Melania Trump's jacket that said, "I really don't care, do you?"

Ryan

I hate the name Ryan, but it's nothing personal. I simply hate *Saving Private Ryan*, the movie.

A private is a soldier of the lowest rank, so who in their right mind would wanna save him? Go save a general or a colonel or somebody who could move you up a level. Just because private Ryan owes you a hundred bucks, there's no guarantee that by saving him you'll get your money back. What if he's still broke? At least if he dies, you'll get your money back by pigging out at his wake. Yes, I'm morbid, but so what? When it comes to money, I don't fuck around.

Saving a private instead of a lieutenant is like saving a janitor instead of the president. Do you think that's a good movie plot? Let's imagine: In the last scene, the secret service is ushering janitor Ryan with a dustpan in his hands inside *Air Force One*, while the president of the United States is gagged and tied up on the floor of the Oval Office. The president sees how dusty it is under the sofa and realizes Ryan is a slacker who failed to run a Roomba and neglected to clean the bathroom. That suddenly explains the stinky toilet the president assumed was Hilary's undigested burrito from the night before. To sum up: not a blockbuster worth seeing. But I'd watch the hell out of a movie called *Saving Ryan's Privates*, which would be about saving Ryan from getting circumcised at a bris . . .

My former coworker Ryan was also a private because he was a very private person who reveals nothing about himself. In the two years working with him I learned one thing about Ryan: his name was Ryan. Asking him questions was a tedious task, as his replies were like my United MileagePlus account—not a single point in sight.

In my opinion, the word "private" is simply a term for "a boring loser with nothing to say." What are you trying to hide, Ryan, by not sharing anything about yourself? Unless you killed five people, put their bodies in your freezer, and now you occasionally make beef Stroganoff out of them, nobody gives two shits about your life. But because people are narcissistic (like I've mentioned many, many times throughout this book), they believe that the world revolves around them and that by being "private," they are interesting and mysterious. What's so interesting or mysterious about a fifty-year-old man in menopause who only talks about work and deadlines? Me, at work I hate talking about work; I love talking about people behind their back, especially about Ryan. For instance, "Ryan has spinach stuck in his teeth—so don't tell him," or "Ryan just microwaved fish. What an asshole." Was that mean of me to say? Sure. But who the hell microwaves FISH in the office? That's why you don't tell Ryan about spinach in his teeth—to get back at him...

Ryan told me on April 15th, "Jeremy, the deadline for filing taxes is today. Did you file yours?"

I said, "TAXES? I barely have time to file my nails."

He said, "When push comes to shove, you have to do it!"

He was right. When push did come to shove, I pushed and shoved him. Down the stairs.

Salvador to Zachary

Salvador
Samantha
Santa
Sara
Snooki
Sonia
Stephanie
Tallulah
Tess
Thor
Tom
Tyler
Unique
Velva
Victoria
Vincent
William
Xanthus
Yolanda
Zachary

Salvador

I hate Salvador Dalí. You've probably gathered from reading this book that I hate lots of people but it's not my fault. If you don't want me to hate you or write about you, stop pissing me off.

Anyhow, Dalí was a sexual assailant. His whiskers were longer than a flight to Australia. He then waxed them until they were stiffer than vodka on the rocks. With those hard whiskers/elephant tusks, Dalí could tickle women's hoo-haws and badonkadonks without their consent. And, like a true pervert, he'd say, "See? Not using my hands. He he he."

The rule of thumb is this: if a person uses "he he he" verbally or through text, that's your cue to run away. Try saying "he he he" out loud in a low voice. DO IT! Does it not creep you out? "He he he" is something that would emerge out of a pedophile's mouth at a playground. Santa's "Ho ho ho" works in a similar fashion because like Dalí he's also a pervert. Read about Santa in the next entry below.

Dalí's bizarre paintings are terrifying, especially *The Persistence of Memory*. In that painting, three teal clocks are melted yet *still* look teal. I don't understand how the color stayed intact. When I tried melting stuff in my childhood, it always came out black and diminished in size, like Ivanka Trump's brain. What does memory have to do with melted clocks? Also, one of those clocks is hung over a dead horse. Who do you think hangs clocks over dead horses? Like I said: a pervert.

Santa

Santa is on my shitlist for lots of different reasons.

First, who but an asshole takes reindeer as public transportation? Sure, the subway in New York City smells like piss, but that doesn't mean animals must suffer just because you like to travel in style. Can't afford a limo or a private jet like Mark Cuban? Take a taxi or fly coach like the rest of us.

Second, who but a pervert enters people's homes through the chimney, and why if not to get frisky? Santa must be wearing SKIMS in order to shove his ass through those tight holes. He works one day a year, so there's plenty of time to exercise and lose weight, but he's too lazy to drive a mile to Equinox. He thinks since dad bods are in season, he can get away with his beer belly. I'm not fat-shaming Santa, but if he continues eating like a pig, he soon won't fit through the chimney and children will spend Christmas "presentless." Actually, just as well. Santa's presents have become boring and unoriginal. I mean how many oversized hoodie blankets and vibrators does one person need?

Unlike children (because they can't talk or simply stupid), famous singers give Santa clues about what they need, but Santa is too fainéant to listen. For example, all Mariah Carey wants for Christmas is "you," and that is another facelift. "I'm Dreaming of a White Christmas" is a white-supremacist song by Stacey Dash. In "Feliz Navidad," José/parrot/broken record is showing Santa he only knows nineteen words and needs a Merriam-Webster. Besides, why should I wait an entire year for one measly present when I have my boyfriend's credit card, Amazon Prime, and free two-day shipping?

Last, how come a creepy trespasser in an unflattering red outfit who enjoys lap dances from little chillens decides who's naughty and who's nice? If you need someone's opinion about your behavior, don't ask Santa, ask your therapist.

Let's boycott/girlcott Christmas and celebrate Chanukah instead. One, it's fun to pronounce—chun-OOka and it rhymes with hooker/bazooka. Two, it's observed for eight days, so it's eight times more festive than Christmas. And three, with all the Christmas trees still alive, a) we'll finally oxygenate the troposphere, b) beavers will have extra timber to munch on, and c) IKEA in Paramus, NJ will never again run out of dressers. Most important, with all this extra wood, the paper industry will thrive and my books will continue getting printed, and like narcissistic turds that you all are, you will continue buying them. HOHOHO.

Samantha

I hate that Samantha and Samuel can both be shortened to Sam, but Assabi and Assad can't be shortened to Ass. That's discrimination. That aside, my eight-year-old niece Samantha is driving me crazy. She never shuts up, and don't quote me but I wish there were long ads in between her conversations . . . *and* subtitles. WTF is RIZZ?

Sam saw me reading *The Hobbit* and asked whether the book was about Lil' Kim (whose height is 4' 11"). Two years prior, as we sat down watching *Beauty and the Beast,* Sam wondered if the movie was about Beyoncé and Jay-Z. When Sam heard "Papa's Got a Brand New Bag" by James Brown, she said, "Mr. Brown is announcing his engagement to Deidre Jenkins!"

I understand that her pea-size brain is still developing, but I don't want Sam to grow up as dumb as her uncle and assume the worst. Just because Sam looks like her neighbor instead of her father, I don't want Sam to assume it's a bad thing—at least she's got some friendly neighbors. And just because she plays guitar, I don't want her to hope she'll end up snorting cocaine and crystal meth and lose her teeth by the time she's twenty-seven. She's not special like Amy Winehouse.

"Guncle Jeremy," she told me last week, "I think the reason Lindsay Lohan developed a Greek accent was because she overloaded on Greek food while in Mykonos."

I said, "Well, Sam, Vanessa Paradis has the biggest hole in her mouth, but that doesn't mean she's consuming food with holes—like bagels, onion rings, and Swiss cheese. Jussy Smollett is a dimwit for staging his own 'hate crime,' but I don't surmise it's because he devoured stupid foods—like gluten-free pasta and Hawaiian pizza. And Salma Hayek speaks with a Mexican accent, but I don't automatically assume she went to Puerto Vallarta and ate a Mexican."

Sara

Sara was the name of my grandmother. You couldn't take her anywhere because she had to use the restroom every five seconds. Don't imagine a nice bathroom either. It was in Kazakhstan, a land of squat toilets, which are nothing but a ditch in the ground with flies buzzing all over the place.

I said, "Grandma, why do you frequent restrooms more often than Renée Zellweger frequents plastic surgeons? You've squatted so many times, Arnold Schwarzenegger is jealous of your glutes. You can probably kick a kangaroo to death."

She said, "I have an overreactive bladder."

I said, "Grandma, it's you who's overreactive. The last time I checked, *you* needed to use the restroom, not your innards. Bladders are basically inflatable balloons, and bladders don't think, akin to Lena Dunham."

Grandma said, "That's what the condition is called, *an overactive bladder.*"

I said, "Grandma, whenever I'm hungry, I don't say my stomach wants to eat. And whenever I steal money from my mom's purse, I don't say my hands did it. I say it was my brother. So admit it, Grandma: You consume more water than your body needs."

She said, "I don't wanna get dehydrated."

I said, "Look at camels, Grandma! They can go for a week without water."

She said, "But I'm not a camel!"

Her two humps said otherwise, but what was the point of arguing?

Snooki

Do you know why Snooki's tan is darker than the Chilean sea bass? When Snooki was six months old, she was adopted from Chile. Don't confuse Chile the country with Chili's the restaurant. They both are technically the same, but only at one of them you will get the bill, and some good mugging at the other.

Chile is a remarkable country though. I've never been myself, but unlike you, I am not ignorant and have looked it up. There are over 2,900 volcanos in Chile, and some of them are more active than John Cena at the gym or your bowels after some questionable Chinese. Because of the volcanos, earthquakes are so constant that cream in your coffee immediately turns into butter. Lava leaves so much red on the ground, you think you're in the state of Alabama.

Did you know that Chile is so narrow you could easily mistake it for the George Washington Bridge and pay the toll by mistake? Chile is also very long and hot like Liam Hemsworth.

But my favorite part about Chile is its national dance, the Cueca, which reenacts the courting ritual between a rooster and a hen. Unlike other more complicated dances such as the Tango, Kuchipudi, or synchronized swimming, in Cueca all you have to remember is that the rooster humps the chicken at the end.

Sonia

Here's my friend Sonia's Instagram bio: "I'm the leader of a group of tree preservationists, and we chain ourselves to trees so they won't get felled. I'm also a mother, a sister, and an aunt."

Look, I admire her passion for protecting trees, and I understand why she's bragging about it, but how is being a sister an accomplishment? *Clearly* you're someone's sister—if you have a fucking sister. And how's being an aunt an achievement? Your sister did all the schtupping!

In the same vein, the former Fox News host Megyn Kelly could've written in her bio: "I'm jealous of Meghan Markle and Prince Harry so I won't stop tweeting about them. I'm annoying, stupid, anti-feminist, and white." Yeah we know.

If you're more boring than Alaska and have nothing else to say, don't post your family tree on social media expecting praise. Do you want to gasconade about your accomplishments? Then *accomplish* something. When the greatest entrepreneur of all time, Donald Trump, couldn't afford to pay the bills, he went bankrupt, and he achieved it eight times and as humble as he is, he never bragged about it.

My advice? Forget about flora and fauna, and allow the wildlife to do all the work. Squirrels—because they're stupid—forget where they bury their acorns and that's how millions of oaks get planted yearly without your help. If you consider yourself an activist, be *active*—go marching or protesting. Chaining yourself to wooden tables at Crate & Barrel and Christmas trees will only make you an attractive ornament, especially if you have big boobs.

Stephanie

My friend Stephanie told me she'd lost twenty pounds by "eating clean." What does it even mean? Is she somehow insinuating that the reason Jason Momoa has gained weight is that he eats out of garbage cans like a freegan?

Who the fuck are freegans, you're wondering? Well, kids, freegans—or dumpster divers—despise capitalism and consumerism. They eat out of garbage cans and squat in unoccupied buildings to save on rent. If freegans could turn their heads 270 degrees, they'd be pigeons.

Garbage-eating sounds exotic, but squatting is not because I hate freeloaders. The reason I don't have children is not because I'm infertile, and if I were I could adopt, foster, or kidnap—a galore of choices. My main problem with ankle-biters is that they live rent-free. In other countries, mainly in Asia and South America, their youngsters fish, drive pedicabs, and advance their careers through various sweatshops.

But in the States, kids aren't required to work because we're too prosperous a country. For that reason, Republicans are against raising the federal minimum wage as Americans already make too much cha-ching. I say we should decrease it even further for our kids. Then, parents will start making less moolah, and children will be forced to get jobs, causing education to dwindle and the economy to tank. Everybody wins!

Tallulah

Tallulah isn't a name—it's a song two goatherds yodel to each other on top of the Swiss Alps: "Ta-da-lu-la-lah . . . ya-hoo." Then they find each other and make love. If you don't believe me, good for you—as I just made it up.

Of all Tallulahs, I love Tallulah Bankhead the most because we have a million things in common. Like me, she was taaaaaalented. Her talent was acting in dramas and you have no idea how dramatic I am. More often than not I cause a scene out of thin air—no scenery needed. Like me, Tallulah hated every name and called everyone "Dah-ling." If she were alive today, I'd like to think that she'd call Senator Mitch McConnell "Douche-ling," and Mike the Situation "Trash-ling."

Like me, she despised the Republican Party, she loved the cocktail hour, and she attended wild sex parties. Rumor has it she slept with women too, and that's where our similarities end . . .

Tess

My friend Tess works in interior design—she's a surgeon—and she's helped thousands of women fix their interior. I don't know about you, but I'm not crazy about boob implants. To sell those, Tess won't tell you you're paying thousands of dollars to gain ten pounds. Instead, she'll say you're getting breast *augmentation*. Such eloquent, sesquipedalian, narcissistic words are the reason you're getting stuffed with silicone on a surgical table. Don't fall for that.

If someone tells you to "coalesce into consummation," they want to "bang" you. And if you've heard that your "flatulence is deleterious," it means your "fart stinks." Finally, if you're told you're an "impecunious grimalkin," that means you're a "broke bitch."

Tess is allergic to nuts, which is ironic because her eyes are almond-shaped. She can't have peanuts, tree nuts, and men's nuts (she's a lesbian). The only nut she can eat is a donut. She once told me, "Did you know that peanut is not a nut but a legume?" in a snooty tone like she's seen a top-secret document from Pentagon. Anyone with ears has heard about the whole peanut/legume thing, so why state the obvious? I never say sentences that are understood like, "Sam Smith is gay" or "New York City is expensive" or "Tess, I know you look like a donkey, but do you have to smell like one too?" It's not a joke. Tess refuses to wear deodorant because most of them contain aluminum. But just because there's aluminum in deodorant, it's not an excuse to have pungent armpits with worse odor than the durian fruit. If I want something stinky, I'll go play with my nephew.

Thor
(Scandinavian for Thot)

Thor is a buff, hammer-wielding god. Traditionally gods are almighty but ugly, but Scandinavian gods are hot and multilingual. Yet my superintendent Thor can barely put two English words together. One time I asked him to come up with his hammer and nail a few things, he misunderstood, stayed home, and nailed his wife instead.

In Germanic mythology, Thor is grand and beautiful, yet still a total baby. Thor gets into these tantrums and starts throwing lightnings and thunderstorms for stupid reasons, such as when his diaper is wet or when another person unfollows him on Instagram. Yet because he's a baby, he is still cute and clumsy and wobbly, and once in a while electrocutes himself with an unplugged iPhone charger.

My friend Thor is neither a God by nature nor a baby by nurture. (What does that mean? It's for me to know and for you to find out.) Thor once told me that he tried "the napkin test"—comparing your teeth to a napkin—and determined his teeth were yellow. Thor lives in the desert so no wonder he's dehydrated and delusional. I told him, "Skinny bitch, I mean Thor, I *also* did the napkin test—with a *brown* napkin—and my teeth never looked better!"

Why do people do this to themselves and compare their teeth to a napkin or eat Tide pods or throw freezing-cold water on themselves? Look, if you want to torture yourself, ask ISIS to waterboard you. Sure it sounds brutal, but at least you'll stay hydrated and, unlike Thor, will stop doing stupid things after watching TikTok videos.

Tom

I hate Tom Cruise because his last name came from cruising guys at a local gym. I don't hate him because he was cruising, I'm simply jealous of his shortness. At exactly five feet, he can give blowjobs without kneeling, which saves him time and also doesn't put pressure on his knee joints, while the rest of us go through life suffering.

When I worked at a restaurant (I'm a trained chef, after all), Tom, the pastry chef, was the most annoying person you ever met . . . at that restaurant. Even more annoying than my mom on two martinis telling me how much she regretted not using a condom the day my brother was conceived. The snooty Tom acted like he was the best baker in the tri-state area, always bragging about his "bread holes." He explained that when the yeast gobbles on starch, it releases some gassy gas that gets trapped by gluten (a protein in the flour), and that creates "air pockets." More holes in the dough mean softer, stretchier bread. He'd bring a loaf after loaf, boasting, "Did you see how big my holes are?"

"Yes," I'd repeat time after time. "The Moon called. It wants its craters back."

Don't you find it narcissistic that Tom takes all the credit when no credit is due? The yeast does all the work by munching on the starch, gaining weight, and sacrificing their figures so people could enjoy a toast in the morning. What if some of the yeast wants to go on a keto diet but can't? Tom doesn't care about the yeast because he's selfish. He's never even asked if the yeast was hungry in the first place. After feasting on the starch—to create "air pockets"—the yeast starts farting to create gas. I find it hard to fart on cue, yet the yeast does it without so much as eating a can of black beans. Maybe they're like my uncle whose flatulence is as expected as tornadoes in Kansas. However, after all the work the yeast puts in, Tom gets the praise, and I find it unfair. When I want acknowledgment for my baking, I always join the yeast and add some of my own farts into dinner rolls. And the holes in those rolls—oooh Mama—are some of the "hole-iest" holes in the whole round world. That's what work of a true giver looks like. And unlike Tom, I've never bragged about it. Until today.

Tyler

Do you know Tyler and Cameron, the Winklevoss twins? I deduced that Winklevoss is a Dutch last name, after hearing my friend Petronella from Amsterdam sing a lullaby to her baby:

> Vinkle, vinkle, vittle star
> How I vonder voss you are
> For you never shut your trap
> You my vittle stupid brat

Or something to that extent. I mean, it's often hard to understand Petronella because she even laughs with an accent. But Petronella also brought up a very good point: the Winklevoss twins must have terrible oral hygiene or otherwise their last name would have been Winklefloss.

The reason I bring up the Twinklesons is because I once stayed at their mansion in LA and I have pictures to prove it.

If you're wondering how in the hell I ended up rubbing elbows with celebrities, let's just say I know some powerful people in Hollywood (and—not related—some very slutty ones in West Hollywood). Before entering the Wrinklevons's house, I had to sign an NDA, so my lawyers suggested I speak in code with anything related to their estate.

The Vinklesons's house is located somewhere up the Hollywood Hills, sandwiched between Keanu Reese's Pieces's house and Leonardo DiGiorno's. There are two floors, five bedrooms, a movie theater, and seven bathrooms, and I did coke in all of them—because why not? I also may or may not have pooped on the lawn to mark my territory. As with every house on the Hills, the house came with an infinity pool, which is slang for "a large bathtub with water dripping down the sides." And what is infinite about it is water: it keeps dripping and dripping . . . while the rest of LA is dry and on fire, not unlike my sister-in-law's pussy after giving birth to six.

The highlight of the Twattersons's house was its kitchen: it was enormous and beautiful—like a groomed King Kong—and I fell in love. Marble countertops, top-of-the-line appliances, Wüsthof knives. As a trained chef, it's my dream to have a fabulous kitchen. The kitchen is where I'm in charge, and not only because I have a cleaver in my hands that can cause some serious damage. Plus I have a black belt from Express that can leave your ass redder than Tennessee. By the way, the only difference between chefs and serial killers is that we chefs at least know how to spatchcock. And how to season.

I fell into deep depression upon my unwilling return to my "flat" in New York City, and I'm not being British. It's just my apartment, compared to the Tweetersons, was flat and uninspiring. The kitchen was teeny and full of cockroaches, and my infinity bathtub would often flood the apartment downstairs, though sometimes on purpose. I've learned my lesson: Never stay at a rich person's house. These days I only become friends with people who are broke and ugly so when I come home at the end of the day I feel better about myself. No, I don't care about your personality whatsoever. If I invite you over for dinner it's because you're very homely but still deserve a nice meal.

By the way, I hate twins as I am jealous of their telepathic abilities. Tyler could tell Cameron, "Quick, think of a communist country that starts with Chi and ends with pollution." And Cameron would reply in Chinese, "中国，你个白痴."

Speaking of China—you'd assume with 1.3 billion people, China would have the most twins on the planet, but you'd be wrong. In Benin, West Africa, there are 28 twins for 1,000 citizens—the highest in the world. When you walk around Benin, you feel horrible, thinking that so many people here look alike. No, you're not a racist—they are actually twins.

But I refuse to make fun of Benin's twins because Benin is where Voodoo originated, and I don't want the Benins to put a spell on me and turn me into JWoww or something worse—like a Honda Civic.

Unique

Naming your baby Unique won't make it unique. Are you expecting a miracle after giving birth? Then order Ozempic—so you could finally lose that pregnant mama muffin.

"Unique" names such as Unique, Ariel, Case (a case of what?), Windy (how many miles per hour?), Panda (from which zoo?), or Azure (a shade of blue) are child abuse. Karma—akin to the writers of *New Girl*—doesn't have a sense of humor. So your baby Case will end up a total nutcase, and Ariel will have one leg like a mermaid. Windy will be loud and cold, and Panda will be black and white—and hairy. And Azure will look like a genie and everybody will start asking her for wishes.

Don't fuck with karma, either, or your baby Hero will become the biggest pussy; your boy Israel will move to Palestine; and your daughter Plain will have fifty-three teeth and all of them wooden—nothing plain about that. Keep in mind, though, that every time Plain quaffs a bottle of red wine, the wood in her mouth will expand and turn into a red dresser—and you'll get yourself the world's first "Cabinet" Sauvignon.

Velva

(I don't know a single person named Velva.
I just wanted to vent about someone/anyone.
So if your name is Velva, you're welcome.)

The name Velva is a hop, skip, and margarita away from being miswritten as Vulva. As you may know, autocorrect is stupid. Whenever I text and say FUCK it changes it to DUCK and whenever I text NJ it changes it to NO. Try writing Velva and see what happens . . .

Anyhow, I feel like there's nothing more embarrassing than texting someone for the very first time and writing, "Hi, Josh, this is Vulva McDonald from Tinder," and hitting send. Then you wonder for hours why he hasn't responded, so you reread your text and try again: "Hi, Josh, this is Volvo McDonald from Tinder—not Velva. It's Vulva!" In the end, don't blame autocorrect—blame your parents for awarding you with this name.

Forget Tinder. You'll become Vulva at Starbucks and everywhere else when they ask you, "What's the name on your order?" And keep in mind, Velva will be misspelled on your passport* too by a lazy USPS worker who gives two shits about your name. So change Velva immediately to a name that's boring and impossible to misspell, such as Vera, Mia, or Lucy. Look, sometimes it's better to be boring than being called Vulva.

Thinking out loud, Velva could also be miswritten as Valve, and you don't know whether to kiss her or to hit her with a wrench.

* Speaking of passports, have you tried getting your passport photo taken lately? You'll find a sign on the window that says: YOUR PHOTO IN JUST ONE HOUR!

JUST one hour??? They make it sound like they're doing you a favor. Since when does it take an hour to take a single picture? How lazy are they? And when the picture gets printed, you somehow always come out looking uglier than an Irish Wolfhound as Instagram filters aren't allowed. I think passports should have no pictures at all.

Victoria

Victoria is a dumb name because I figured out her secret a million years ago. Victoria's Secret was founded in the 1970s, so how's that a secret that she had gonorrhea and snorted cocaine? Everybody did. If I were her, I'd have changed my name from "Victoria's Secret" to "Everybody at Studio 54 Knows."

Let's discuss Queen Victoria of England, who also had secrets. Did you know that Queen Victoria of England proposed to her husband Albert? Which, in my useless opinion, makes perfect sense. According to the oil paintings of her I found online, she was homely and, therefore, a tad eager to settle down. The kicker is, Albert was her first cousin, and I suspect that's where the royal family's peculiar fascination with inbreeding began. After Albert died, Queen Victoria mourned his death by wearing black for the rest of her life. In my opinion, it actually has nothing to do with his death, but because black is slimming and she'd gained lots of weight by spending years feasting on fish and chips and washing that down with a copious amount of gin.

I have a friend Victoria, who *also* has secrets. What's up with this name and all the secrets, I wonder? Anyhow, Victoria is single and ready to mingle, which is why she stuffs her boobs with socks for a bigger cleavage, which does attract more dates. I don't know about you, but fooling people by stuffing yourself with apparel is mean and dishonest. The only time when stuffing yourself with apparel is allowed is when you want more clothes but can't afford them. So you go to a dressing room at Zara and stuff every crevice of your body with garments. Before you go, ask Kim Richards, Farrah Fawcett, or Megan Fox how to safely shoplift. As you're leaving the store and the alarm goes off, you'll be patted down—so you'll get a free massage out of it too!

Vincent

I hate Vincent Van Gogh.

In ten years, he painted not one, not two, but *thirty-six* portraits of himself. Don't compare those to selfies. A selfie takes half a second, but Vincent spent months in front of a mirror. If he was cute, it'd be another fucking story, but he was not. Not at *all*. Thirty-six dumb portraits of his Dutch mug and not a single picture of his sausage. Look, if I ever wanted thirty-six Dutch mugs, I'd stop at a souvenir shop in Amsterdam.

William

My friend William is a waxer, and he's very annoying.

One time while waxing my butt, he asked me, "How's the job hunting going?"

I said, "Ouch—it hurts! The job hunting is going well, and I have an interview tomorrow."

He said, "Don't forget to wear 100 SPF sunscreen. You know, the kind that leaves you really pale?"

I said, "Why should I wear sunscreen to a job interview? Is my employer . . . the sun?"

He said, "The whiter you are, the better your chances you'll get hired."

"William, that's fucked up."

"No, Jeremy, that's the USA."

I hate William for bring up uncomfortable subjects like racism. Over the years he's brought up everything, from death to diarrhea to sexual assault to mass shootings to the way my weight fluctuates from month to month. One time I confided in him that I've tried cocaine a few times and his reaction was overdramatic: "Ewwwww, Jeremy. Drugs are so gross!"

I said, "You wax butts for a living! How drugs are grosser than that?"

He said, "Well, I wax butts but I don't sniff them! I'm not a dog!"

His foul breath and drooling mouth said otherwise, but unlike him I don't bring up uncomfortable subjects (such as halitosis or hypersalivation)—because I'm classy and only discuss these subjects behind your back.

Xanthus

I don't mind the name Xanthus when I see it written on a piece of paper, but I hate it when I try to pronounce it. My mouth becomes so puckery, it's as if I'm chewing on a lemon.

Names Xanthippe, Xochitl, or Xerxes are similarly irritating. I hate it when parents get annoyed if I mispronounce Alethea, Balthazar, or Thanasis. Chill the fuck out. *You're* the ones who gave your child such impossible-not-to-mispronounce names. There are numbers, punctuation marks, and silent letters in way too many names for my liking.

The name X Æ A-Xii is pronounced *Ex Ash A Twelve*. Twelve is how many toes it has.

The name La—a is pronounced *Ladasha*. She was born in a coma and will never have a period.

And the name Ailbhe? You have to say *AL-va*.

So if I ever have a child, I must be creative too to stay trendy. My kid's name will be written as 7/\|\|3 but pronounced—Jane.

Yolanda

Names starting with Y are all plagiarized: Yasmin is a knock-off from Jasmin, Ysobel from Isobel, and Yuliana from Rudy Giuliani.

Yolanda, Yoshi, Yona, and Yoko are the worst of them all. I hate it when people start their sentences with "Yo," as it sounds "street" and unprofessional, and I hate it when people talk as if they spent their entire life in Alaska talking to bears. For example, "Yo, you're so stupid" sounds very condescending. But "You look beautiful" does not, because it doesn't start with "Yo."

However, name your baby Yolanda only if it comes out uglier than a Christmas sweater and you want to divert people's attention away from the fact you've birthed a Mowgli lookalike.

Zachary

Words take energy to pronounce, and unless I have an Adderall for lunch, I won't remember a long name like Zachary. The only long thing I'll tolerate is a long flight to London, and do you know why? British people are classy and aristocratic, and they love drinking. While alive, Queen Elizabeth enjoyed a cocktail of Gordon's gin and Dubonnet before lunch and a glass of champagne after dinner—every single day. That's why at ninety-five, she was fit as a fiddle, classy as a harp, and wrinkly as an accordion—all because she drank. Then her doctor told her she had to stop to look good for her jubilee, and what happened? She passed away. I hope you catch my drift.

More importantly, I love how British people utilize tag questions, which are basically statements that don't require a response. Like, "Julian Assange's butthole will sure be sore in prison, wouldn't it? And speaking of buttholes, Senator Ted Cruz is such an ass, isn't he?" Since the answer isn't required, you conserve your energy, and that's very classy, in my opinion. What I'm trying to say is, Zachary, change you long, annoying name so I don't have to drink a Red Bull every time I open my mouth trying to pronounce it.

I know I'm jumping from place to place the way Steve Bannon jumps from one drug dealer to the next, but do you know what else is classy? Martinis, English tea sandwiches, and *Breakfast at Tiffany's*. Do you know what's trashy? Pumpkin spice lattes, Doritos, and *The Bachelor*.

Speaking of *The Bachelor*. Watching a show about thirty-seven whores and a lady-killer* is as entertaining as a vacation in Afghanistan. Every week, the bachelor gives the women roses with razor-sharp thorns. Several of the contestants have gone home in an ambulance, drunk and bleeding. Have you seen the contestants, by the way? They're so annoying and neurotic, I'm surprised they're not taken away in straitjackets.

* By the way, the real lady-killer was Terry Nichols, who was involved in the Oklahoma City bombing in 1995 that killed 168 people. He'd received 161 life sentences, plus 9,300 years without parole. I know he's made a boo-boo, but he won't see his friends for over 10,000 years. Don't you think he won't learn his lesson in the first thousand? The real question is, what stops him from playing dead 161 times and then get out and start bombing again? I say execute him by making him watch all twenty-five seasons of *The Bachelor*. He'll kill himself.

Messages to People I Hate

Mother

I understand you LOVE being a grandma and all, but from now on, for every picture of my brother's children that you send me, I'm going to send you a picture of something similarly ugly in return—so get prepared to see lots of Republican senators, and pictures of my father.

Father

Darling, it's high time you moisturized that visage! Your latest Instagram post makes my face look like a baby's bottom in comparison. Honestly, I wouldn't be surprised if squirrels started mistaking you for a giant acorn. Remember that time in Central Park? The one where you resembled a particularly knobby oak tree so much that a squirrel decided to stage a sit-in on your forehead? I nearly choked on my croissant. You're more bark than beauty, my dear...

My Ex

(Which one? All of them.)

My undying affection for you compels me to suggest these exhilarating activities:

1) Embrace the unknown: Close your eyes and take a leisurely stroll across I-95.
2) Urban exploration: Take the train to Newark. At night.
3) Embrace the exotic: Acquire a tarantula as a captivating new companion.
4) Embrace the aromatic: Indulge in a sensory experience at the renowned Port Authority Bus Terminal's restroom facilities.
5) Challenge the status quo: Express your unwavering allegiance to the Democratic party at a gathering of white supremacists.

Gian

There are lots of Gians I've met over the years, so you have to figure out whether I'm talking about you or not. I can give you a clue: You are Californian who once lived with a girl whose teeth were the shade of something a dog buries after going number two.

I hate you for three simple reasons:

1) Your mac and cheese taste better than mine. What's your secret? It's very gooey, and cheesier than the movie *Twilight*. Speaking of which, I wasted two hours watching Kristen Stewart moseying around with a face more sour than rhubarb. My lips still pucker thinking about it. I couldn't find the plot, so I finally called the cemetery and ordered one.

2) People treat you with respect, yet even AI devices such as Alexa and Siri talk back to me. For example, the other day I asked Siri the meaning of "floccinaucinihilipilification." She said, "Floccinaucinihilipilification is the action or habit of estimating something as worthless. Worthless. Like this book."

3) I hate your clothes because you only wear black and white. What's up with that? It's not like they are flattering colors. If you wear black and white, at least make it look expensive. Skin a skunk or a panda. The upside: you'll get petted, and who doesn't enjoy unwanted affection?

Messages to People I Love

So strange . . .

can't think of
anyone.

The end

Names Mentioned in This Book

A: Adam, Alex, Alexa, Alexander, Amber,
Andrea, Andrés, Angela, Anna, Anne, Anu, Ashlyn
B: Bibi, Billy, Brie, Britney, Brooklyn
C: Cedric, Cesar, Charley, Christina,
Claude, Clint, Crystal, Curtis
D: Dan, David, Delia, Dick, Divanna, Don, Donald
E: Elizabeth, Elle, Emily, Eric, Eve, Ezequiel
F: Felicia, Felicity, Florina, Franzy, Frida
G: George, Georgia, Gian
H: Henok, Hudson, Hung
I: Isaac, Ivy
J: Jeff, Jeremy, John, Jonathan
K: Kaitlin, Karl, Karen, Katie, Kenya, Kevin, Kris
L: LaToya, Laura, Leah, Leonardo,
Lilly, Liza, Louis, Lydia
M: Marc, Mary, Matthew, Melania, Michael, Mimi
N: Nathan, Nelsie, Nick
O: Ocean, Orlando, Osama, Oscar
P: Patrick, Pearl, Phillip, Pierce, Pinocchio
Q: Quigley, Quin
R: Ramy, Reign, Rhett, Rosa, Rudy, Ryan
S: Salvador, Samantha, Santa, Sara,
Snooki, Sonia, Stephanie
T: Tallulah, Tess, Thor, Tom, Tyler
U: Unique
V: Velva, Victoria, Vincent
W: William
X: Xanthus
Y: Yolanda
Z: Zachary

Acknowledgments

My publisher insisted that I have an "acknowledgments" page. Look, this is not a magazine article or a research paper and nobody *helped* me write it. Me, myself, and I did all the fucking work. Acknowledging anyone makes no sense, especially since I've finally lost any remaining friends because of this shady, fabulous book. But I have two whole pages to fill, so . . .

Thank you, Ramy. But here's a tip, next time when writing a foreword, be MORE spiteful and disrespectful. Nobody can gain anything from being NICE! I was nice once and you know what I gained? Fifteen pounds.

Thank you, Nelsie, for editing my book/teaching me how not to write/so on and so forth/yada yada yada. You're absolutely the most handsome man on Earth, and I love you! (Oh, sorry, Nelsie, I got bored with you and was writing how I feel about my husband.)

Speaking of which, thank you, Andrés, for adopting me from the pound and making an honest ~~dog~~ woman out of me.

Thank you, Johnny, my lawyer who, like everyone else involved in this book, was hard to work with. When I had envisioned the cover of my book—to match the book's narrative—wanted to see Rowan Atkinson, Susan Boyle, or another ugly face—but Johnny said I would be sued and that it was a very stupid idea. So I asked the cover artist to put Johnny's wife on the cover. Who's stupid now, Johnny?

To the book interior design team: Next time, please make the font BIGGER so that hateful words like "hate," "disgusting," and "asshole" stand out. I spent two years writing this book and I want people to *really* understand how I feel about them.

OK, I'm done thanking.

Antoni Porowski, text me. Let's go for lunch at the Manhattan Detention Complex to chat with the former Subway spokesperson Jared Fogle and also with Ghislaine Maxwell, for whom I have some "minor" questions.

(Did any of you get it? "Minor" questions? . . . Because Jared Fogle and Ghislaine Maxwell had sex with . . . minors? Oh, right, you bought my book—you're stupid—so never mind.)

Lastly, there are not 111, but 116 people in this book. I added five more because I have that much anger, and my therapist advised me to release my anger openly—so you're welcome.

You ugly hag, Betty Davis, I still hate you.

—Joan Crawford

About the Author

Jeremy Taylor lives in West New York City, NJ and is the author of:

Diary of a Mad Gay Man
The Cornerstones of Happiness
Smart Casual and Other Expressions I Hate
The Girl and Apple Martinis
Puss on the Loose
Noodles with Grandma and Other Stories from Our Homestead in Kazakhstan

Books that make him laugh are:
I Hate Everyone Starting with Me and *Diary of a Mad Diva* by Joan Rivers | *My Horizontal Life: A Collection of One-Night Stands* by Chelsea Handler | *Are You There God? It's Me, Margaret* by Judy Blume | *R Is for Ricochet* by Sue Grafton

Some of his favorite TV shows are:
I Love Lucy, Crazy Ex-Girlfriend, Kim's Convenience, Schitt's Creek, Friends, Sex and the City, Broad City, Emily in Paris, The Good Place, Young & Hungry, Workin' Moms, Desperate Housewives, The Kardashians, Foundation (UM ... HELLO!).

WWW.JEREMYTAYLOR.ONLINE

www.instagram.com/jeremy.taylor.ny

www.x.com/jeremytaylor_ny

www.youtube.com/@jeremytaylor9037

www.ingramcontent.com/pod-product-compliance
Lightning Source LLC
Chambersburg PA
CBHW030451100526
44580CB00005B/76/J